QUALITATIVE TEXT ANALYSIS

SAGE has been part of the global academic community since 1965, supporting high quality research and learning that transforms society and our understanding of individuals, groups, and cultures. SAGE is the independent, innovative, natural home for authors, editors and societies who share our commitment and passion for the social sciences.

Find out more at: **www.sagepublications.com**

QUALITATIVE TEXT ANALYSIS

A Guide to Methods, Practice & Using Software

UDO KUCKARTZ

Los Angeles | London | New Delhi
Singapore | Washington DC

Los Angeles | London | New Delhi
Singapore | Washington DC

SAGE Publications Ltd
1 Oliver's Yard
55 City Road
London EC1Y 1SP

SAGE Publications Inc.
2455 Teller Road
Thousand Oaks, California 91320

SAGE Publications India Pvt Ltd
B 1/I 1 Mohan Cooperative Industrial Area
Mathura Road
New Delhi 110 044

SAGE Publications Asia-Pacific Pte Ltd
3 Church Street
#10-04 Samsung Hub
Singapore 049483

Editor: Katie Metzler
Production editor: Sushant Nailwal
Copyeditor: Kate Harrison
Proofreader: Anna Luker Gilding
Indexer: Avril Ehrlich
Marketing manager: Ben Griffin-Sherwood
Cover design: Francis Kenney
Typeset by: C&M Digitals (P) Ltd, Chennai, India

Library of Congress Control Number: 2013939874

British Library Cataloguing in Publication data

A catalogue record for this book is available from
the British Library

ISBN 978-1-4462-6774-5
ISBN 978-1-4462-6775-2 (pbk)

Table of Contents

List of Figures

List of Tables

About the Author

Udo Kuckartz is a Professor of Educational Research and Social Research Methods at Philipps University Marburg, Germany. He teaches courses on qualitative and quantitative methods, general research designs, and mixed methods research. He also taught at the Free University Berlin, the Technical University Dresden, and the Humboldt University Berlin. He received his Master's degree in Sociology and Political Science from RWTH Aachen, Germany. With a doctoral dissertation on "Computer and Verbal Data," he obtained his Ph.D. in Sociology from the Technical University Berlin, Germany. Some years later he earned his habilitation, a second qualification common in many European countries, in Educational Research from the Free University Berlin.

He authored 17 books and more than 180 articles in journals and as contributions to books. Most of his books are focused on qualitative and quantitative methodology, e.g. textbooks on qualitative evaluation, on-line Evaluation, computer-assisted qualitative data analysis, and an introduction into statistics. Since the 1980s, he has worked on computer-assisted methods of qualitative data analysis (QDA). In connection with his doctoral dissertation on computer and verbal data, he was a pioneer in the field of QDA-software and developed the software MAX (later winMAX, which is known worldwide today as MAXQDA).

He is currently working on his 18th book, a textbook on Mixed Methods. At Philipps University Marburg, he founded the Magma Research Group, which organizes the annual "CAQD – Computer-Assisted Qualitative Data Analysis" Conferences.

Dr. Kuckartz' applied research focuses on environmental issues, particularly on environmental attitudes and behaviour, as well as perceptions of climate change. He has served as a leader for many nationwide surveys on environmental attitudes on behalf of the German Federal Ministry for the Environment, Nature Conservation, and Nuclear Safety. He has also completed other research projects in this field for the UBA, the German Environmental Protection Agency, and for the German Federal Agency for Nature Conservation.

Acknowledgements

This book is the result of many seminars and workshops that I gave at the Philipps University of Marburg, where I am teaching since more than ten years, and other places around the world. To that extent, I am indebted to many students and colleagues who have helped me to develop the concept of systematic qualitative text analysis and to examine its practical application and implementation. For the constructive discussion of the manuscript in its various stages, I am especially grateful to Stefan Raediker, Claus Stefer, and Thomas Ebert and to Uta-Kristina Meyer, Julia Busch, and my wife Anne Kuckartz. Mailin Gunkel, Gaby Schwarz, and Patrick Plettenberg have eagerly helped with the layout, bibliography, and technical drawing. A special thanks goes to John Creswell, who has encouraged me again and again to translate my books, which were previously published only in German, into English and thus make them known in the English-speaking world.

As always, the writing of this book was a long process, from recording my first ideas to submitting the final camera-ready draft. It was great fun and often challenging and I thank everyone who has supported me.

Preface

This book is the result of a long-standing plan of mine to write a hands-on guide to systematic analysis of qualitative data. As a university professor, I observed how unsure graduate students and doctoral candidates felt when analysing qualitative data. At a loss, they searched for an appropriate analysis strategy and, specifically, for methods described as accurately as possible as well as techniques they could apply to the practical implementation of their analysis. This book will help to satisfy this need. It presents the central steps of the process of qualitative text analysis in a straightforward way and describes three main methods in detail: *thematic*, *evaluative* and *type-building analysis*.

Qualitative text analysis, as described in this book, derives from many sources – thematic analysis, grounded theory, classical content analysis, and others. It is a sort of *hermeneutical-interpretive informed systematic analysis*. In European countries, very often, the term 'qualitative content analysis' is used for that kind of analysis. In the Anglo-Saxon world, however, the method 'content analysis' is strongly associated with the quantitative paradigm. There, the term 'qualitative content analysis' seems like a contradiction in itself. To avoid misunderstandings, I will therefore use the term qualitative text analysis in this book instead of 'qualitative content analysis'. Three distinct forms of qualitative text analysis are described in detail in this book, with particular regard to complex types of analysis and the presentation of results. The possibilities for qualitative text analysis have expanded greatly because of modern computer technology; thus, this book will also present possibilities for practical implementation using QDA software (QDA stands for Qualitative Data Analysis).

The three methods described in this book, 'thematic text analysis', 'evaluative text analysis', and 'type-building text analysis', represent three independent approaches that can also build on each other. Uwe Flick (2006, pp. 295–298) differentiates between methods of qualitative data analysis that use 'coding and categorizing' on the one hand and 'sequential analysis' (broken down into 'conversation and discourse analysis' and 'narrative and hermeneutic analysis') on the other hand. The three methods presented in this book belong to the first group, i.e. *category-based methods for the systematic analysis of qualitative data*.

Like Clive Seale and others (Seale, 1999b; Seale & Silverman, 1997), this book strives for methodological rigour in qualitative social research. An accurate description of the analytical approach and the recognition of the existence of quality standards are, in my opinion, as essential to qualitative text analysis as to any analysis method in the social sciences. With the new techniques of computer-based analysis, ranging from different methods of coding and re-finding, linking and writing notes to complex modelling and visualization of qualitative data analysis, powerful tools are available to increase the quality of the analysis. The closer proximity to the data, better accountability, transparency and documentation are likely to increase the credibility of qualitative analysis and thus, their general appreciation in the scientific community. For this reason, this book assumes that modern computer techniques will be used and includes them as an integral part of the presentation of methods.

The aim of the book is to provide a hands-on description of the qualitative text analysis approach, using the example of the analysis of qualitative interviews, and more specifically of guideline-structured interviews. Theoretically, the methods presented are suitable for other data types such as narrative interviews, observation protocols, visual data, images, documents, etc., but they must be adjusted accordingly. The three methods presented here are not intended to form a rigid, constricting concept. These methods can be modified, expanded and differentiated according to the approach adopted for actual analysis in a research project. Here, I refer to the position expressed by Huberman and Miles regarding the flexible application of evaluation strategies:

> Data analysis is not off-the-shelf, rather it is custom-built, revised, and 'choreographed'. (quoted by Creswell, 2003, p. 142)

Thus, this book does not present a one-size-fits-all approach to qualitative data analysis, rather methods of analysis are presented, which have to be adapted to the specific situation of a research project.

The book is constructed as follows: Under the heading, 'Analysing Qualitative Data – But How?', Chapter 1 presents essential foundations and argues the importance and the central role of the research question. Chapters 2 and 3 then turn to qualitative text analysis in the strict sense. The second chapter traces the path from different 'sources' like grounded theory, thematic analysis and classical quantitative content analysis to qualitative text analysis, after which the basic concepts and the general process of qualitative text analysis are shown in the third chapter. The fourth chapter represents the core of the book, in which three methods of qualitative text analysis are described in detail. Chapter 5 focuses on the possible assistance computer software can provide throughout the entire analysis process, from transcription to presentation and visualization of results. The following chapter, Chapter 6, is devoted to issues of quality standards, creating the research report, and documenting the analysis process. My original plan envisaged the book with the chapter on quality standards before the chapter 'Qualitative Text Analysis using Computer Assistance'. This proved to be unpractical because the way in which the software itself is used is relevant when assessing the quality of qualitative text analysis. Thus, one would have had to take frequent reference to something which was only described in the subsequent chapters, so that ultimately it seemed sensible to move the chapter on quality standards back.

In the Internet era, it has been found that texts are perceived more as a hyper-text rather than read sequentially or in their entirety. People often search very selectively for the information they need. This book does not follow this trend; rather, it has a linear structure, i.e. it is designed so that individual sections build on one another and should therefore be read consecutively.

Udo Kuckartz, Marburg, April 2013

PREFACE

1

Analysing Qualitative Data – But How?

In this chapter, you will learn more about:

- The difference between qualitative and quantitative data.
- The ambiguity of the term 'qualitative data analysis'.
- The relationship between qualitative, quantitative and mixed methods research.
- The importance of the research question in an analysis.
- The need for methodological rigour in qualitative research.

1.1 Qualitative, Quantitative – A Few Clarifications

What do the terms 'qualitative data' and 'quantitative data' mean? While the term 'quantitative data' is directly associated – even by laymen – with numbers and statistics, and likely with costs in economic fields, the term 'qualitative data' is not equally self-explanatory, as it has very different meanings in various scientific disciplines as well as in everyday life. In human resources, for example, it entails areas such as employee satisfaction, motivation, and work environment as opposed to quantitative (hard) data, such as personnel costs, headcount, etc. For geographers, the number of inhabitants in various communities represents typical quantitative data, while classifying a municipality into zones involves qualitative data. In psychology, qualitative data often refers to data of the scale type nominal or categorical, i.e. actual data from the field of standardized (quantitative) research. There you will even find textbooks that introduce the term 'qualitative data' in the title, but which actually involve quantitative analysis methods for categorical data.

This book is based on the following pragmatic definition of quantitative and qualitative data:

> Numerical data, or numbers, are considered quantitative data. Qualitative data are more diverse in contrast and can include texts as well as images, movies, audio-recordings, cultural artefacts, and more.

Despite the multimedia revolution that took place in the last decade, and despite the noted epochal shift towards the visual in our culture, text is still the dominant type of qualitative data in social sciences, psychology, and education. The methods of qualitative data analysis described in the following are originally designed for the data type 'text' and texts will be used in the examples shown. Theoretically, the methods can be transferred to other types of qualitative data such as images, movies, audio-recordings, etc.

Unlike the attitude often found in textbooks on social research methodology, I do not view qualitative data as inferior to other (quantitative) types of data. There is no hierarchy of analytical forms similar to that of scales – which includes nominal, then ordinal, and finally interval scales on the highest level. 'Real science' does not begin with numbers, quantification, and statistical analysis of data. One glance at other scientific disciplines proves this point. In many branches of science, including geophysics and medicine, scientists work with non-numerical data, such as in the field of advanced medical imaging techniques (MRI, NMRI, etc.). Qualitative data are by no means a *weak* form of data; rather, they are a *different* form that requires different, complex and systematic analysis.

An interesting aspect in this context has been introduced by Bernard and Ryan (2010, pp. 4–7). They have pointed out the ambiguity of the term 'qualitative data analysis', which is immediately apparent when the three words 'quality', 'data', and 'analysis' are linked together in different ways. While qualitative data *analysis* refers to the analysis of qualitative data in the above sense of texts, images, films, etc., *qualitative* data analysis can mean the qualitative analysis of data of any kind, that is, both qualitative and quantitative data. Differentiating between data and analysis results in the following four-cell table (according to Bernard & Ryan, 2010, p. 4)[1]:

The chart presents two expected and two unexpected cells. The upper left Cell A and the lower right Cell D appear well known to us: Cell A includes the *qualitative analysis of qualitative data* in the form of hermeneutical analysis,

---

[1]The table is based on the earlier differentiation by Bryman (1988), which differentiated between qualitative and quantitative *research*, not *data*. Bryman called the cells B and C 'incongruent'.

Table 1.1 Qualitative and Quantitative Data and Analysis (Bernard & Ryan, 2010)

Analysis	Data	
	Qualitative	Quantitative
Qualitative	A	B
	Interpretive text studies. Hermeneutics. Grounded theory, etc.	Search for and presentation of meaning in results of quantitative processing.
Quantitative	C	D
	Turning words into numbers. Classical content analysis, word counts, free lists, pile sorts, etc.	Statistical and mathematical analysis of numeric data.

grounded theory, or other qualitative analysis techniques. Cell D, *quantitative analysis of quantitative data,* is also familiar to us. This involves the use of statistical methods, i.e. the typical process for analysing numerical data.

The table also includes two cells that we may not necessarily expect, namely the *qualitative analysis of quantitative data* (Cell B) and the *quantitative analysis of qualitative data* (Cell C). The latter may include the analysis of word frequencies and word combinations. The qualitative analysis of quantitative data (Cell B), which involves interpreting quantitative data, begins when the statistical methods are calculated and the results are presented in the form of tables, coefficients, and parameter estimates. At this point it's time to identify and interpret the meaning of the results. Without this interpretive step, the quantitative analysis of raw figures remains sterile and literally *meaningless.* As Marshall and Rossman emphasized, the interpretive act is inevitable:

> The interpretive act remains mysterious in both qualitative and quantitative data analysis. It is a process of bringing meaning to raw, inexpressive data that is necessary whether the researcher's language is standard deviations and means or rich descriptions of ordinary events. Raw data have no inherent meaning; the interpretive act brings meaning to those data and displays that meaning to the reader through the written report. (2006, p. 157)

Bernard and Ryan's differentiation makes it clear that the type of data does not necessarily determine the type of analysis. If you move away from such a strict connection between data type and type of analysis, it is clear that both a quantitative analysis of qualitative data, as well as a qualitative analysis of quantitative data, are possible. Thus, there is no reason to suspect a deep divide between the qualitative and quantitative perspectives. In everyday life, as in science, human beings have a natural tendency to combine methods. We always try to keep both perspectives – the qualitative and the quantitative aspects of social phenomena – in mind.

1.2 Qualitative, Quantitative and Mixed Methods Research

You would expect that a book on the analysis of qualitative data would not only define the terms 'qualitative data' and 'quantitative data', but would also give a definition of the term 'qualitative research', which goes beyond 'collection and analysis of non-numeric data'. There are many relevant definitions and many attempts to compare quantitative and qualitative research.

Flick's textbook, *An Introduction to Qualitative Research* (2006), begins with a note on the dynamics of qualitative research:

> Qualitative research is an ongoing process of proliferation with new approaches and methods appearing and it is being taken up by more and more disciplines as a core part of their curriculum. (p. xi)

In the latest edition of their handbook on qualitative research, Denzin and Lincoln emphasize the diversity of qualitative research, which shows how impossible it is to provide a 'one-size-fits-all' definition:

> The open-ended nature of the qualitative research project leads to a perpetual resistance against attempts to impose a single, umbrella-like paradigm over the entire project. There are multiple interpretive projects, including the decoloniz-ing methodological project of indigenous scholars; theories of critical peda-gogy; performance (auto) ethnographies; standpoint epistemologies, critical race theory; critical, public, poetic, queer, materialist, feminist, reflexive, eth-nographies; projects connected to the British cultural studies and Frankfurt schools; Grounded Theorists of several varieties; multiple strands of eth-nomethodology... (2011, p. xiii)

Qualitative research includes a variety of individual, sometimes exotic meth-ods and techniques. In the early 1990s, Tesch tried to organize the diversity of approaches to qualitative research in a mind-map style table. The result was a collection of nearly 50 different qualitative approaches, trends and forms of analysis, ranging from 'active research' to 'transformative research' (Tesch, 1992, pp. 58–59). Tesch arranged the various approaches in a *cognitive map* and differentiated between the approaches according to whether the research inter-ests were based on: a) the characteristics of language; b) the discovery of regu-larities; c) understanding the meaning of the text or the act; or d) depends on reflection.

It seems that almost every author of a qualitative methods textbook feels com-mitted to creating a new systematization of qualitative approaches. The results of such systematization vary: almost a decade later, Creswell's differentiation, for example, is completely different than Tesch's. Creswell distinguishes between five different (main) approaches of qualitative research: 'narrative research', 'phenomenology', 'Grounded Theory research', 'ethnography' and 'case study' (Creswell, in Miller & Salkind, 2002, pp. 143–144). Tesch's differentiation is geared primarily towards the researcher's interests while Creswell focuses on epistemological and pragmatic aspects. Thus, Creswell does not aim to construct a comprehensive systematization; rather, he examines the most frequent approaches used in practice.

While this is not the place for a synopsis of the great diversity in systematization, the variety of qualitative approaches explains why there is no underlying, unified theoretical and methodological understanding (see Flick, 2007a, pp. 29–30). Accordingly, the definitions of 'qualitative research' vary greatly. Some elements, including case-orientation, authenticity, openness and integrity, can be found in almost every definition. It will suffice here to refer to Flick, von Kardorff, and Steinke's (2004, p. 9) 12 characteristics of qualitative research practice:

1   Spectrum of methods rather than a single method
2   Appropriateness of methods
3   Orientation to everyday events and/or everyday knowledge
4   Contextuality as a guiding principle
5   Perspectives of participants
6   Reflective capability of the investigator
7   Understanding as a discovery principle
8   Principle of openness
9   Case analysis as a starting point
10   Construction of reality as a basis
11   Qualitative research as a textual discipline
12   Discovery and theory formation as a goal.

In textbooks on research methods, however, you will find a comparison of quantitative versus qualitative research. Oswald argues, in his handbook article, 'What is qualitative research?' (Oswald, 2010), that qualitative and quantitative methods are located on a continuum, i.e. there are similarities and overlaps, and a variety of useful combinations between them. According to Oswald, there are qualitative characteristics (usually called categorical data) in quantitative research and the results of statistical analysis are *interpreted*. This argument is very similar to the aforementioned argument by Bernard and Ryan. Conversely, qualitative research often includes a quasi-quantification, which is reflected in the use of terms such as 'frequently', 'rarely', 'usually', 'typically', etc. The following instructive description of the difference between qualitative and quantitative research results from Oswald's considerations:

> Qualitative research uses non-standardized methods of data collection and interpretive methods of data analysis, where the interpretations are not only related to generalizations and conclusions, as in most quantitative methods, but also to the individual cases. (Oswald, 2010, p. 75; translated from German)

What already shines through in Oswald's position, namely that qualitative and quantitative methods are not mutually exclusive, has been the focus of the discourse on *mixed methods*, which has developed into a sort of movement in the Anglo-Saxon realm, particularly in the US, over the course of the last decade. The mixed methods approach is – according to its protagonists – a new and modern methodological approach, which tries to overcome the old duality of approaches in a new, third paradigm. Scholars such as Creswell, Plano, Tashakkori, Teddlie, and many others have formulated the mixed methods approach in great detail and developed a variety of precise design proposals for mixed methods research.[2] These authors' proposals for *practical research* projects are extremely interesting and relevant in many scientific disciplines. *Methodologically*, Udo Kelle's work to integrate methods should be taken into account within this context (Kelle, 2007b). While the mixed methods approach requires pragmatism (see Creswell & Plano Clark, 2011, pp. 22–36), Kelle's approach (2007b) is epistemological, beginning with the controversy regarding the role of explanation and understanding that shaped the humanities and natural sciences for more than 100 years. His concept of the integration of methods is methodological and he attempts to substantiate the combination of methods on a much more profound level. Kelle goes back to the dawn of empirical social research and the qualitative-quantitative controversy, and asks how it is possible to develop empirically-based theories in the social sciences and arrive at a concept of 'causal explanation', which, in principle, we already find in Max Weber's research (see Kuckartz, 2009).

1.3 The Challenge of Analysing Qualitative Data in Research Practice

The methodological orientation of empirical research in the social, educational, health, and political sciences and to a lesser degree in psychology has shifted since the early 1990s – qualitative research, which lagged behind even

---

[2]Tashakkori and Teddlie's *SAGE Handbook of Mixed Methods* (2010) provides a good overview of the many facets of the mixed methods approach.

in the 1980s, has establish itself and is increasingly popular today, especially among young scientists. Meetings and conferences, such as the Berlin Methods Meeting[3] or the International Congress of Qualitative Inquiry,[4] are evidence of the great resonance that qualitative research has produced world-wide today.

Along with this shift towards qualitative research methods, the amount of appropriate methods literature that is available has increased, especially literature in English. Most of this literature on qualitative methods and mixed methods is mainly concerned with data collection and design, while questions of qualitative data analysis are given less attention. If one considers, for example, the latest edition of Denzin's and Lincoln's 'The SAGE Handbook of Qualitative Research' (2011), one finds only three contributions that deal explicitly with data management and models of analysis.[5]

In an online German doctoral forum, I recently read a graduate student's plea for help:

Hello,

I really wanted to create an online survey for my MA thesis (it's about differentiation/separation in the relationship of grown-up children to their parents). Since my constructs are difficult to understand, my supervisor recently said: Have you ever thought about tackling the whole research project qualitatively and conducting interviews?

　　Hmm. Now I am rummaging through a lot of literature, mostly from the social sciences. But I simply cannot find anything tangible for analysing qualitative data. This is all very vague. And I would really like to report some results at the end. Feeling a little hopeless at the moment. Can anyone here give me any tips?

Regards,
Dana

This grad student, Dana, is right: A tangible and concrete method for analysing qualitative data is not easy to find. And that is where this book comes in – our

---

[3]Website: www.berliner-methodentreffen.de

[4]Under the direction of Norman Denzin, this conference is held annually in Urbana, IL (USA), see www.icqi.org.

[5]Whereas in the past there was little special literature on qualitative data analysis available – like Dey (1993) or Miles & Huberman (1995) – the situation has changed in the last few years. See for instance, the books of Gibbs (2009) and Bernard & Ryan (2010), which deal with a variety of methods for analysis.

aim is to show ways in which qualitative data can be analysed and methodology controlled in a systematic manner. To collect qualitative data is interesting and exciting and it is usually feasible without major methodological problems. The difficulties with which researchers are faced in the early stages of a project are more related to field access or the researcher's own behaviour in the field, rather than the methods employed to collect the information in the narrower sense. But what comes after you have collected the information, recorded interviews with a recording device, for example, and after you have transcribed the interviews, or written field notes or collected data in the form of videos?

Students are not the only ones who feel unsure at this point in the research process and avoid the risks associated with qualitative research because the analysis process and the individual steps of the evaluation are not described precisely and in enough detail in the literature and are therefore difficult to carry out. Even in major projects funded by national agencies, there are often very imprecise descriptions of the approach to data analysis. Researchers often use empty phrases to merely describe that they 'based their analysis on the Grounded Theory', 'interpreted according to Silverman', 'on the basis of qualitative content analysis', or by 'combining and abbreviating different methods'. A precise, well-understandable representation of the procedure is often omitted.

On the other hand, the mentality 'anything goes'[6] can often be found in the discourse on methods of qualitative data analysis: Researchers who read qualitative methods texts and come to such a conclusion believe that they can more or less do what they want, make glorious interpretations, let their own imaginations and associations have free rein, without the danger of strict methodologists rejecting them and/or putting them in their place. They can even call on the constructivist and postmodern positions encountered in the discussion of the quality standards for qualitative research, which emphasize that the social world itself is constructed cognitively and that multiple worlds and world-views exist side by side; thus, the question of universal and objective quality standards would become obsolete. Such positions are not shared in this book. It seems to me that Seale's position of a 'subtle realism' (Seale, 1999b) is convincing – in the discourse on the quality of qualitative research, Seale pleaded pragmatically (based on Hammersley's work (1992)) for a compromise between the two extremes, namely between the adherence to the rigid rules of classical research concepts (objectivity, reliability, validity) on the one hand and the rejection of general criteria and standards on the other. Promoting the formulation of appropriate quality standards and precise descriptions and documentation of analytical procedures (see Chapter 6) would undoubtedly

---

[6]'Anything Goes' by the American philosopher of science Paul Feyerabend (1975) was not meant as a licence to allow researchers to do anything they wanted methodically speaking, but as an invitation to use creative methods in their research.

increase credibility and reputation when addressing a 'sceptical audience' (Seale, 1999b, p. 467) as well as research institutions.

1.4 The Importance of the Research Question

The pivotal point of any research project is the *research question*: What would you like to achieve through the research project? What is the specific problem that you would like to explore? Why and with what practical purpose? What type of investigation should be conducted to obtain information about the research question, and what methods are most suitable?

Miller and Salkind distinguish between three basic types of research, which are reflected in corresponding designs: *basic, applied,* and *evaluation research* (Miller & Salkind, 2002). Although basic research is ideal for experimental methods and testing of hypotheses, in general all three types of research may work with both qualitative and quantitative methods. According to Miller and Salkind, the various directions of research questions constitute the differences between the methods:

> They are not another way to answer the same question. Instead, they constitute a relatively new way to answer a different type of question, one characterized by a unique approach with a different set of underlying assumptions reflecting a different worldview of how individuals and group behaviour can best be studied. (Miller & Salkind, 2002, p. 143)

Other textbooks distinguish between four types of studies: exploratory, descriptive, hypothesis-testing, and evaluative studies (see Diekmann, 2007, pp. 33–40). Both qualitative and quantitative methods can be used in all four types of study, and it is also possible to combine both methods within one type of study. The proportion of qualitative methods is different for the different types of studies. While mostly qualitative methods can be found in exploratory studies, descriptive studies, which will give the most generalized overview possible, rely on more quantitatively oriented survey research. The starting point for all four types of study is the *research question*. Without such, research is hard to imagine. Because no matter whether you are planning a master thesis, or a dissertation, or a research proposal for which you wish to receive external funding, the first step is always to face the challenge of drawing up an exposé, a research plan, or research proposal, in which the presentation and discussion of the research question plays a central role.

In *formulating the research question* you should always ensure the theoretical background and reflect on your own prior knowledge, then ask yourself: How much have I thought about the field of research? What other research already exists? Which theories seem to have explanatory power regarding my research question? What prejudices do I have myself and what prejudices are common among the scientific community of which I am a part?

To ask such questions is not in contrast with the idea of openness that is characteristic of qualitative research. The common assumption that researchers can be a 'tabula rasa' or a 'blank slate', able to devote themselves to a research subject entirely without prior knowledge, is an illusion (see Kelle, 2007a, 2007b). Prior knowledge is always a factor, as the researcher's brain is never 'empty'. Even if after well-founded consideration, you choose not to refer to existing research results because you would like to approach your research question and approach the field 'without prejudice', you should reflect on your reasons for doing so and record them on paper. The mere reference to scholars who recommend such a theory-free and unprejudiced approach is not suffi-cient to justify it; instead it requires reflection regarding exactly why such a theory-abstinent approach for answering your research question is appropriate and why this promises better results. We often find statements referring to the grounded theory, noting that it is counter-productive to read books on the topic of research as a research methodology. This discredits qualitative approaches. In the various approaches of today's grounded theory, this misunderstanding, found in the early reception of texts on grounded theory itself (Glaser & Strauss, 1998), has been corrected (Cisneros-Puebla, 2004; Kelle, 2007a, 2007c).

Of course, there are situations in social research in which it is advanta-geous to gain experience in the field first. For instance, anyone who wants to observe and experience how homeless people live should not simply plan to sit in the library reading the sociological and psychological literature on homeless people. On the other hand, it is hard to imagine that anyone who wants to analytically explore the causes of right-winged thinking in adoles-cents would consistently ignore all of the research literature that already addresses that very problem. In this book, the position is taken that it is wise and necessary to start with the existing research when exploring social phenomena. I agree with Christel Hopf, who encouraged researchers to delve through the current state of research on the chosen topic:

> Therefore, there is no reason to prematurely view the independence of your own judgment pessimistically, thus destroying many opportunities for gaining insight that are associated with theory-driven, empirical studies based on exist-ing research. (Hopf & Schmidt, 1993, p. 17)[7]

---

[7]Translated from German.

1.5 The Need for Methodical Rigour

What is the justification for analysing qualitative data in a systematic manner and according to strict rules? Does such an approach hinder the creativity and openness of qualitative methods? In qualitative research since the mid-1990s, issues of quality and validity have been discussed intensively. Three principal positions are taken regarding the acceptance and transferability of existing quality standards for quantitative research:

a) Universality: The same standards are valid for qualitative research as for quantitative research.
b) Specificity: Specific standards that are appropriate must be formulated for qualitative analysis.
c) Rejection: Quality standards are generally rejected for qualitative research.

Flick (2006, pp. 379–383) adds a fourth position, namely, that researchers should be able to answer the question of quality beyond the formulation of standards, such as in the form of total quality management, which takes the entire research process into account. For the general discourse on the quality standards for qualitative research, it will suffice here to refer to relevant contributions (Flick, 2007a; Seale, 1999b; Steinke, 2004). At this point, the topic will be considered with a focus on the method of qualitative text analysis, and the second of the above positions will serve as a basis – namely that specific, appropriate standards for qualitative research must be formulated and not simply carried over from quantitative research. Inspired by the psychological test theory, standards for objectivity, reliability and validity have been established in quantitative research, which can be found in almost every textbook of social research methods. These quality standards are based on the scientific logic of measurement and more oriented towards measurable variables (e.g. reliability coefficient). Standards for the quality of qualitative research, however, cannot be based on calculations and measures, as the data for such a calculation is missing. Thus, following Flick (2006), the standards themselves must be more process-oriented.

In recent years, increased efforts have been made to canonize and 'precisify' qualitative and mixed methods research procedures[8] and to discuss aspects of quality (Flick, 2006, pp. 367–383). In particular, the work of Clive Seale has been given a lot of attention. Seale and Silverman (1997, p. 16) pleaded, as shown above, in favour of ensuring rigour in qualitative social

---

[8]A good example is the work of John Creswell concerning the different designs of mixed methods research.

research and the construction of quality criteria. Does this mean that we have to take over the logic behind the quality standards of quantitative research and apply fixed technical evaluation instruments? Seale's position of 'subtle realism' is a middle road beyond loose acceptance or rejection of the classical quality standards. The standards within quantitative research cannot be carried over directly to qualitative research.

Qualitative research is carried out in natural settings and differs from the hypothetico-deductive research model. There, the focus is on testing hypotheses and the goal is to find correlations and create causal models that can be generalized. Qualitative research can generalize, too, but this is its not main purpose. In particular, the broad generalization that is inherent in the research logic of the hypothetico-deductive model, is a foreign concept in qualitative analysis (Seale, 1999b, p. 107). Ultimately, the goal of the hypothetico-deductive model is to discover patterns and even laws with universal and long-term validity, while in qualitative research, in particular in the theory-building Grounded Theory, the goal is to establish middle-range theories.

What, specifically, are the reasons to proceed with methodical rigour when analysing qualitative data? Five aspects are important arguments for systematic kinds of analysis and qualitative text analysis in particular:

- Against anecdotalism: Systematic analysis avoids the trap of 'anecdotalism', since all of the data are included in the analysis and not only selected quotes are presented.
- Transparency: A detailed and transparent description of the analysis process increases the general understanding for the scientific community and other interested readers.
- Trustworthiness: Trust in the researchers and the results of their research is increased when specific standards are followed.
- Reputation: Methodological standards allow qualitative researchers to improve their reputations beyond their scientific communities.
- Increase interest and acceptance of funding institutions.

Methodological rigour also deals with the problem of quantification in qualitative research:

> Yet, as I showed in the last chapter, numbers have a place within qualitative research, assisting, for example, in sensitive attempts to learn lessons in one place that have relevance for actions and understanding in another place. There is a variety of other uses of numbers which can enhance the quality of qualitative research ... (Seale, 1999b, p. 120)

As a result of his very instructive overview of the benefits and use of numbers in qualitative research (see Seale, 1999b, pp. 119–139), Seale formulated the principle of 'counting the countable'. Numbers can assume different functions; they can represent not only simple frequencies or percentages, but also be used for more complex statistical calculations, such as cross-tabs with chi-square test or cluster analysis. They can clarify arguments and support theories and generalizations. Seale's emphasis on 'avoiding anecdotalism' expresses the importance of using numbers quite concisely (Seale, 1999b, p. 138).

2

The Building Blocks of Systematic Qualitative Text Analysis

In this chapter, you will learn more about:

- The fundamental problems associated with understanding texts.
- Hermeneutics that classically deals with the interpretation of written text.
- Different methods for qualitative text analysis that work with codes and categories, namely:
  - o Grounded Theory as a method, in which codes and categories play a central role;
  - o classical content analysis and its origins which go back to the German sociologist Max Weber in the early twentieth century; and
  - o criticism of classical content analysis and how to conceptualize qualitative content analysis.
- Other approaches to qualitative text analysis as described in textbooks on social research methods.

A variety of methods and techniques for analysing and interpreting text have been developed in various disciplines, e.g. in social science, political science, psychology and educational science. These approaches have been worked out more or less precisely. Some of them, like Grounded Theory are well known and recognized globally, while others are primarily used in only one discipline or only one country.

These methods are used like bricks to build the approach of systematic qualitative text analysis presented in this book.

We will outline four such approaches in the following sections, including:

- classical hermeneutics
- coding in Grounded Theory
- content analysis and qualitative content analysis
- research practice as described in textbooks.

These approaches employ different forms of coding and are based on various theoretical assumptions; however, it would go beyond the scope of this book to present and discuss them all in detail. All of the methods presented in this chapter, however, are based on working with codes and categories. The only exception is classical hermeneutics – the art and science of text interpretation – which does not work usually with codes. The chapter starts with presenting major ideas of hermeneutics that are also relevant for all kinds of text analysis in the social sciences. Hermeneutics is not a *method* in the same sense as Grounded Theory or content analysis but it deals with the entire framework of the process of analysis and interpretation and can therefore be stimulating and inspiring for the development of systematic qualitative text analysis.

The section thereafter deals with Grounded Theory and particularly with the way Grounded Theory works with codes and categories. This serves as an example of developing codes in a multi-step process that starts with simple 'open coding' and ends up with the discovery of 'core categories' and building a theory.

A kind of counterpart to this approach of discovery is the object of the next section: content analysis, a classical concept of text analysis that can look back on a hundred-year history. In content analysis, it's not the discovery of codes and the coding scheme which is the centre point of the analysis process, but the application of the coding scheme on a well-defined number of texts. Content analysis is primarily focused on transferring the texts with the help of the category system in a numerical data matrix. This has often been criticized and led to the demand for the integration of qualitative elements. The idea of a qualitative content analysis tries to overcome the weaknesses of the classical content analysis and integrates steps of interpretation into the analysis process.

This chapter ends with a look into textbooks that deal also with methods for the analysis of qualitative data. In these textbooks, examples of good research practices can be found and advice is given how to perform the analysis of qualitative interviews and qualitative data in general.

This chapter aims to outline the main features of the different methods. I do not intend to present an exhaustive description and have included references to relevant literature, which enable the reader to explore the individual methods further, if desired.

2.1 Classical Hermeneutics

How can you analyse a text in context of social research? Without even *understanding* a given text, you can analyse only its characters and words – or its syntactic properties – in order to find out more about the length of the text, the number of words in the entire text or the number of different words used, the average length of sentences, the number of subordinate clauses, and so on. In short, this is all the information that you would receive when you choose 'Properties > Statistics' in a word processing software. However, if you wish to analyse the semantics within the text, you will have to address the question of how to understand and interpret the text. In everyday interactions, we naively believe that people can innately *understand* each other, as if we could open a newspaper and *understand* an article that refers to the Euro crisis and how European countries are dealing with it. However, at second glance, it becomes clear that real understanding requires a wealth of previous knowledge and other information. First and foremost, we have to understand the language in which people are communicating. If the same newspaper article were written in *Kinyarwanda*, few of us would understand it. In fact, most readers likely do not even know what kind of language Kinyarwanda is![1] However, even if you understand the language, you must also have a good deal of previous knowledge in order to understand what the Euro, the different countries in the EU, and the different currencies are (to continue the above example). Finally, in order to really understand it, you have to know the history of the Euro and be familiar with the aims of having a single currency in the EU.

The more we know, the better we are able to recognize that a text has different levels of meaning. For example, only with previous knowledge on the subject could you recognize that the politician quoted in the newspaper article, who used to be a strict opponent of the financial support for Greece, has now given surprisingly balanced and convincing arguments in favour of the support. Moreover, if you know that that same politician is an active member of the state government, you can assume that that governmental body may be changing their stance on the issue as well.

It is impossible to gain an inductive understanding of a text by itself. Middle Age Biblical illustrations serve as a good example of this: The more you know about the iconography of the time and the better your knowledge of Christian symbolism, the better you will understand a given illustration. This sort of understanding cannot be deduced from the illustration alone, as Christian symbolism goes beyond the illustration – and the Bible cannot be construed inductively based on illustrations of different Biblical scenes.

Before analysing qualitative data, it is important to consider some general thoughts regarding understanding, specifically understanding and interpreting texts. This is often referred to as *hermeneutics*. But what exactly is meant by *hermeneutics*?

---

[1] Kinyarwanda is a Bantu language that is spoken in the Eastern African country of Rwanda and in Eastern Congo.

The term hermeneutics is derived from the Greek word ἑρμηνεύειν (hermeneutike), which means to explain, interpret, or translate. Hermeneutics, then, is the art of interpretation, the techniques involved in understanding written texts. As a theory of understanding, hermeneutics has a long history that extends as far back as the medieval interpretations of the Bible or even to Plato. Within the context of scientific thought, hermeneutics appeared in the late 19th century as leading philosophers, including Schleiermacher and Dilthey, proposed hermeneutics as the scientific approach of the humanities in contrast to the explanatory methods of the natural sciences. Cultural products such as texts, illustrations, pieces of music, or even historical events were to be developed and understood within context. Dilthey wrote that we explain nature, but in the human sciences we have to establish a different methodological foundation based on understanding and interpretation ('verstehen').

The difference between explanation and understanding has been discussed a great deal in theoretical and scientific literature; thus, we will not address it any further here. If you are looking for an instructive text on the topic, see Kelle (2007b), which tries to take a new approach to the old explanation versus understanding debate. Kelle relies on Australian philosopher John Mackie's concept of multiple causality (see Kelle, 2007b, p. 159 referencing Mackie, 1974).

Over time, hermeneutics have evolved – from Schleiermacher and Dilthey to the modern day approaches of Gadamer, Klafki, Mollenhauer, and others[2], there is no single, uniform hermeneutical approach today. Some time ago, Anglo-American philosophers also became aware of hermeneutics through the work of Richard Rorty (1979). For the purposes of this book, we are less interested in the historical, theoretical, and philosophical aspects of hermeneutics and more interested in the guidelines hermeneutics offer for the analysis and interpretation of data collected in qualitative research projects. How do we take a hermeneutical approach to analysing the content of texts? Klafki presented a comprehensible example based on an interpretation of a Humboldt text about how to construct the Lithuanian city school system (Klafki, 2001). In his text, which was first published in 1971, Klafki formulated 11 methodological insights for his hermeneutical approach, which still apply today. Five of the main points are important within the context of qualitative text analysis:[3]

---

[2]Gadamer elaborated a concept of philosophical hermeneutics; in his book *Truth and Method* (2004), he dealt with the nature of human understanding.

[3]This section is based on the ideas presented in Jochen Vogt's lecture, which is available online at www.uni-duisburg-essen.de/literaturwissenschaft-aktiv/Vorlesungen/hermeneutik/main.html (Accessed on 9 January 2011). Vogt examines hermeneutics extensively in his book *Invitation to the Study of Literature* (2008).

First: The conditions under which the text was created

Bear in mind the conditions under which the text you wish to analyse, such as an open-ended interview, was created. Who is communicating with whom and under which circumstances? How much and what kind of interaction the researcher had with the field of research prior to the interview? How would you characterize the interactions between the interviewer and the participant? What are the mutual expectations? What role may social desirability play in the interactions between the researcher and the participant?

Second: The hermeneutic circle

The central principle in the hermeneutic approach is that a text can only be interpreted as the sum of its parts and the individual parts can only be understood if you understand the whole text. You should approach the text with some preconceived notions and assumptions about what it could mean and then read the text in its entirety. By working through the text with an open mind, you will gain a better understanding of it, which will likely change some of your original assumptions.

Any attempt to understand a text presupposes some prior understanding on the part of the interpreter. Klafki noted that reading through the text and/or parts of the text multiple times results in a circular process (Klafki, 2001, p. 145); however, it would seem that a spiral serves as a more suitable illustration since you do not circle back to your starting point. Instead, you develop a progressive understanding of the text.

The hermeneutic circle or spiral is often visualized as follows (Danner, 2006, p. 57):

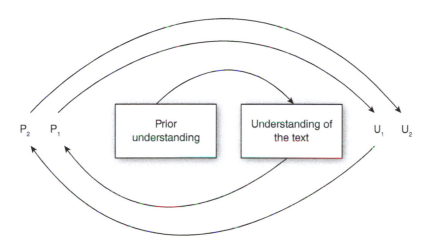

Figure 2.1 The Approach of Hermeneutics (according to Danner, 2006)

Third: The hermeneutic difference

The notion of the hermeneutic difference points to the central problem of all verbal communication, namely that we can only understand texts and communication in general – or think we understand them – through an interpretative process. Initially, everything is foreign to us and we understand to varying degrees; thus, the hermeneutic difference varies. It is at its highest when, for example, we visit a foreign country and cannot understand the language that is spoken, even higher if the character system is foreign to us, and we cannot even look up the unknown words in a dictionary.[4] In everyday communication, the hermeneutic difference seems small or even obsolete. According to Schleiermacher, no hermeneutics are necessary to talk about the weather or when we order 'Five rolls, please' at the bakery. However, unexpected irritations to everyday communication are quite common, too, such as when differences in dialects or accents surface. As Gadamer noted, hermeneutics take place in the grey area between foreign and familiar: 'Hermeneutics are situated in this place in between' (Gadamer, 1972, p. 279).

Fourth: Accuracy and suitability

Hermeneutic approaches attempt to understand cultural products such as texts, pictures, and art. As Mollenhauer and Uhlendorff (1992) emphasizes, they attempt to understand them *accurately*. None of the methods, however, can guarantee *accuracy*. In hermeneutics, it all depends on the *person* trying to understand or interpret something, who always has some sort of preconception about the object or subject at hand. Gadamer stressed that these are 'pre'conceptions or assumptions. Thus, a hermeneutic interpretation that fulfills the criteria for inter-subjective agreement cannot be postulated per se. There is no right or wrong interpretation, rather a more or less suitable interpretation.

In summary, the following five hermeneutic rules apply to qualitative text analysis:

1 Reflect on your own preconceptions and any assumptions you may have regarding the research question.
2 Work through the text as a whole, setting any unclear passages of the text aside until you gain a better understanding of the entire text, which may shed light on the unclear passages.

---

[4]In general, we can differentiate between three forms of hermeneutic differences: linguistic, historical, and rhetorical. The above example is an example of a linguistic difference. Historical difference can manifest itself as a factual or linguistic difference, such as in the form of outdated concepts or sayings, or unknown persons, facts, or situations.

3   Make yourself aware of the hermeneutic difference by asking yourself, 'Does the text contain a different language or culture with which I am unfamiliar?' Try to reduce these differences, such as by learning the new language or finding an interpreter.[5]

4   During your first reading of the text, pay attention to the topics or themes that are important to your research and where they appear in the text.

5   Try to differentiate between the logic of discovery and the logic of application of codes and coding frames. It is something different when you identify topics and categories in the text and index the text with already defined categories, or when you are discovering something new, such as when you identify new and perhaps unexpected information in the text, develop new theoretical ideas and define new codes.

It is often assumed that hermeneutics is a method that only partially corresponds to the scientific demands of inter-subjectivity and validity. This is, however, a very narrow view since hermeneutic methods are indeed a part of empirical research, particularly in proposing hypotheses and interpreting results. Moreover, even strictly quantitative research cannot be conducted without hermeneutic considerations, i.e. without thinking about the meaning of results. Klafki addressed the idea that research questions and research designs always have hermeneutic prerequisites. In the field of education, he noted:

> I suspect that every hypothesis in empirical research is based on considerations that aim at determining the meaning or significance of something and can thus be considered hermeneutical considerations. This does not, however, mean that all empirical researchers would recognize the thought processes leading up to their hypothesis as hermeneutical steps or practice the necessary precision in formulating hypotheses as in hermeneutics. The fact that researchers arrive at hypotheses hermeneutically in empirical research is often overlooked because many professionals in the field already have common preconceptions. For example, they may find particular questions meaningful for a given time period or for their research as a whole because they already have a previous common understanding of the subject. (Klafki, 2001, p. 129)

2.2 Grounded Theory

Anselm Strauss and Barney Glaser's approach named 'Grounded Theory' has attracted increasing interest around the world. In a variety of textbooks – some written individually, some as joint efforts – Strauss, Glaser, and later Corbin,

---

[5]This is true in cross-cultural research, but it can also be useful for research conducted in a familiar environment. Sprenger (1989) tells of a social science project about the use of technology in critical care and how medical experts were invited to help the research team interpret the phenomena they observed, which made a scientific analysis possible.

Charmaz and Clarke developed this approach, in which categories and coding play central roles, (see Charmaz, 2006; Clarke, 2005; Corbin & Strauss, 2008; Glaser & Strauss, 1967; Strauss, 1987; Strauss & Corbin, 1998). Over the course of three decades, Grounded Theory evolved and advanced continuously (see Charmaz, 2011). In the beginning, it was rather formulated as an inductive approach and seemed to promote a more or less theory-less approach: everything the researcher theorized before the analysis ('preconceived theories') was thought to inhibit rather than promote his or her perceptions during the analysis process. Bit by bit, Strauss and Corbin integrated more elements from classical research concepts into the approach. Grounded Theory started in the mid-1960s with Strauss and Glaser's attempt to create a political science manifestation in response to behaviourism and the quantitative mainstream, who had pretty much side-lined the interaction approaches during the politically conservative post-war period in the US. This assumption is supported by Strauss' own retrospective observation that he expressed in an interview with Legewie & Legewie-Schervier:

> In the mid-1960s, we decided to write a methods book. We could already feel the air of change. We wanted to write for the 'kids', as people above the age of 30 seemed to be too committed to other theories. Barney had a hunch that such a book would be well received; I was more skeptical because I was older. The title, 'Discovery of Grounded Theory' (1967), shows what was important to us: unlike in the normal methods textbooks, it was not examining the theory that was important, but discovering and exploring them using the data. *Grounded Theory* is not a theory, but a methodology used to discover the theories lurking within the data. (Legewie & Schervier-Legewie, 2004, p. 51)[6]

Strauss' successive specification of Grounded Theory as a method of analysis also led to controversies between the two founders of Grounded Theory.[7] Kelle provides a basic description of the core of the conflict (2007c). According to Anselm Strauss, a grounded theory consists of categories

---

[6]Translated from German.

[7]The following original texts explain the basic ideas of Grounded Theory: a) Glaser and Strauss (1967) *The discovery of Grounded Theory*. It deals with the first comprehensive portrayal of Grounded Theory, published in 1967, and includes all of the misunderstandings surrounding the theory at that time. b) Strauss (1987) *Qualitative Analysis for Social Scientists*. This text uses course protocols to make Strauss' approach understandable and practicable. However, the text often lacks conceptual clarity. c) Strauss and Corbin (1998) *Basics of Qualitative Research: Techniques and Procedures for Developing Grounded Theory*. This book complements the previous text – Strauss and his co-author Juliet Corbin attempt to systematically define and describe the different tools and methods within Grounded Theory.

and their theoretically meaningful features and hypotheses; in other words, of general connections between categories and their properties. Categories and the coding process are central to Strauss' and Glaser's approach. The careful coding of the data – that means assigning codes to specific phenomena in the data material – is central to Grounded Theory that differentiates between three main types of coding: open, axial, and selective coding.

> Coding is the pivotal link between collecting data and developing an emergent theory to explain these data. Through coding you define what is happening in the data and begin to grapple with what it means. (Charmaz, 2006, p. 44)

Open Coding

Open coding is the process in which you start to investigate, compare, conceptualize, and categorize data. Open coding 'opens' the analysis, you process the data carefully and develop preliminary concepts and their dimensions.

> Initial codes are provisional, comparative, and grounded in the data. (Charmaz, 2006, p. 37)

Conceptual codes and so-called in-vivo codes are applied to the data. Strauss noted that in-vivo codes are terms used by the participants, which the researcher then applies as codes. In-vivo codes enable us to access the participant's perceptions directly, without obstructing them by the theories we develop. Such terms will catch your eye as you interpret the data. For example, in one of Strauss' studies, a head nurse called a staff nurse the 'station's tradition bearer' because her duties included training the new employees and familiarizing them with the station's rules and general operating procedures.

Strauss and Corbin define concepts as 'conceptual identifiers or tags to which specific occurrences, incidents, and other phenomena are assigned'. An example of such an identifier is the label 'Appraisal of Social Loss'. The result of the first step of the analysis is a list of concepts, which can be summarized into categories in the next step. For Strauss, a category is an independent terminological element of a theory; it is a classification of concepts. This classification occurs when we compare concepts with each other and they appear to refer to similar phenomena. In this manner, concepts are grouped together under a concept of higher rank – an abstract concept, called a category, such as 'Caring for Personnel'.

Categories have properties, dimensions and subcategories. Strauss and Corbin define those terms as follows:

Properties: Characteristics of a category, the delineation of which defines and gives it meaning.

Dimensions: The range along which general properties of a category vary, giving specification to a category and variation to the theory.

Subcategories: Concepts that pertain to a category, giving it further clarification and specification. (Strauss & Corbin, 1998, p. 101)

For example, the category 'Caring for Personnel' contains the subcategories 'Professional Calmness' and 'Appraisal of Social Loss'. To a large extent, Strauss uses the terms dimensions and sub-category as synonyms. Sub-categories can also contain dimensions. For instance, the sub-category 'Appraisal of Social Loss' could contain the dimension 'Rationalizations for Loss'.

Creating dimensions is an important part of developing categories. Categories have dimensions, which can be described on a continuum: the level of 'Professional Calmness' and 'Appraisal of Social Loss' can be low or high:

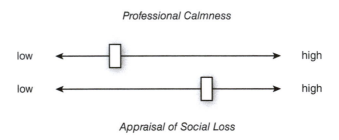

Professional Calmness

low   high

low   high

Appraisal of Social Loss

Figure 2.2 Dimensions of Categories

Hence, the open coding stage of the analysis process consists of conceptualizing the data and identifying and defining the dimensions of categories and their sub-categories. Open coding can be completed in a variety of ways, though Strauss recommends proceeding through the material line-by-line or segment-by-segment.

Codes can be based on single words, complete sentences, passages within the text, or entire documents. If based on documents, the aim is to compare documents as a whole, classifying them according to similarities and differences. In this case, codes would take on the character of 'case variables'. The following example of a category 'observation' with different sub-categories and dimensions stems from a study that Strauss did on working types.

Category	Sub-category	Specific Dimension
Observation	Frequency	often ---------------- never
	Extent	many ---------------- few
	Intensity	high ---------------- low
	Duration	long ---------------- short

Figure 2.3 Dimensions of the Category 'Observation'

Axial Coding

Strauss and Corbin (1998) describe *axial coding* as a special, advanced coding technique that is implemented upon the completion of the open coding process. They defined it as a 'set of procedures in which the open coding categories are put together in a new way based on connections established between the categories. This is achieved by way of a coding paradigm, which contains conditions, context, strategies, and consequences' (Strauss & Corbin, 1998). Thus, axial coding focuses on one specific category and its connections. A heuristic framework provides a general model of operation, in which the categories are examined according to six classes:

1 Phenomena
2 Causal conditions
3 Context
4 Intervening conditions
5 Action strategies
6 Consequences

In this manner, the analysis process achieves a more abstract level and moves into the third form of coding, *selective coding*.

Selective Coding

This is defined as 'the process of choosing a core category, systematically relating all other categories to that core category, validating these connections, and replenishing categories that require further refining and development' (Strauss & Corbin, 1998, 143). This stage of the coding process integrates the entire analytic work that has already been done. The connections between the core category (or categories) and other categories are examined. Dividing the data into groups, allows you to discover patterns and models by observing the specific dimensions within the categories. This corresponds to the multivariate statistical analysis in quantitative analysis; however, the focus here is placed on constructing an *analysis story* rather than on coefficients and significant statistics. Such stories must contain a central category and be ordered in a logical and sequential manner (Strauss & Corbin, 1998).

How exactly does coding and generating codes work? Strauss was not very dogmatic, as he viewed his Grounded Theory style of analysis as one of many possible styles of analysis. By the same token, he stressed the importance of aligning the methods with the concrete question at hand. The specific procedure is less decisive than the goal of the analysis, which is the theory – both generating a theory and evaluating it. This highlights clear differences to, first, a qualitative analysis strategy with a particular focus on description; and second, to the position that seeks to limit qualitative research to exploration and theory generation and maintains that testing of theories is reserved exclusively to quantitative research. Strauss formulated: *Coding within the framework of Grounded Theory is theoretical coding, meaning we work towards developing a theory as we code.*

Yet, the above sentence reveals a problem with Grounded Theory as a method of analysis, namely an inherent vagueness and indefiniteness. How, you might ask, can you simultaneously generate and evaluate a theory based on the same data? In addition, generating theories is not an exact process; it is a mix of intuition, hard work, creativity, solid previous knowledge, and last but not least, coincidence and luck. These characteristics add a dose of vagueness and indefiniteness to the Grounded Theory method of analysis. Coding is an art form in Grounded Theory. Thus, master craftsmen play a significant role. In order to learn their craftsmanship, you have to look over their shoulders and see them at work. The impression that this craftsman-apprentice constellation evokes echoes that of Strauss in the documentations of his seminars found in his central work, *Qualitative Analysis for Social Scientists* (1987).

Therefore, the analysis process according to Grounded Theory is not subject to any sort of strict progression. Strauss argued against systematically employing methodological rules. He is obviously not in the camp of those scholars who raise the demand for methodological rigour. Grounded Theory merely provides guidelines and aids. According to Strauss, coding is data analysis, and analysis is the same as the interpretation of the data. This means that coding is a procedure that takes place throughout the entire research process and not only at one specific point in time or at a specific phase of the process.

In the following, we will attempt to arrange the individual components and method guidelines of Grounded Theory according to the logic of the research process, knowing that the Grounded Theory approach applies especially to circular approaches. The 12 steps described below allow 'regressions' back to previous steps. In spite of the circularity, Grounded Theory begins with a reading of the first text (such as an interview transcript, a protocol, a group discussion, or a field note) and ends with the composition of the research report. Coding evolves from open coding, which opens the work and sort of 'breaks the seal' on the data, to complex axial and selective coding. The three different forms of coding also describe specific sequential phases of the research process, whereby a 'phase', unlike in the strict successive phases within classical social research, can by all means contain circular elements. Obviously, selective coding cannot take place in the first phase of the research process; you must work your way through the open coding phase first.

1 Read the entire text. If working in a research group, all members of the team who will take part in the interpretation must read the text.

2 Previous knowledge about the subject matter to be researched is very important and most definitely welcome. Many research questions can be posed based on general and previous knowledge before you even read and evaluate the first interview. In principle, an analysis using Grounded Theory is possible without previous knowledge, but the outcomes would likely be less sound and you would run the risk of producing results that experts would view as trivial.

3 The actual analysis and interpretation are carried out as a detailed analysis of the entire text's background.

4 The analysis begins with open coding, which includes looking for answers to pointed questions in the text material (see Flick, 2006, p. 300):

What? What is this text about? What phenomenon is addressed?
Who? Who takes part, plays a role? How do the various persons interact with each other?
How? Which aspects of the phenomenon are (not) addressed?
When? *How long*? *Where*? *How many*? *How strong*?
Why? What reasons are given in the text or can be deduced from the text?
What for? What is the purpose, intent?
With what? What means were implemented in order to achieve the goals?

5 The approach is flexible when it comes to modes of analysis. You can begin with a line-by-line analysis at the beginning of the text or choose to systematically examine an aspect that is central to an interview. (Example: Let's look at the first four pages of the text. What do they tell us about the category 'managing emotions'?). Either way, you start the interpretation at the beginning of the text and perform a line-by-line analysis; you do not anticipate the story. The analysis includes the interpretation of what was said using the backdrop of your general, research-oriented, and scientific knowledge and the information to come in the other interview texts. An extensive interpretation using the backdrop of previous knowledge is best carried out in a research group, for, as we all know, two (or more) heads are better than one and a research team may have a corrective function, which helps to minimize misconstructions and false interpretations.

6 Pay attention to 'natural codes', or a participant's noticeable wording. (For example, a patient recounted undergoing a routine cancer examination. Out of the

blue, she was given a very negative diagnosis. In the interview, she said, '...I flipped out'.)

7 The interpretation leads to the discovery of codes (such as 'diagnostic career' or 'medical stations').

The codes in this phase can have various levels of abstraction. Hence, Strauss created the code 'medical funnel', which refers to the phenomenon that people often have to make decisions when they are ill. They can decide whether or not to take medications, agree to an operation, etc. They have less and less room to make decisions as the illness progresses; in the end, decision-making is usually left to the doctors.

Unlike in quantitative research, a passage of text can be assigned multiple codes in Grounded Theory.

8 Any ideas that refer to other passages in the text (or perhaps remind you of the entire text's central theme) can be recorded as memos. Memos serve as reminders for the corresponding pages of the interview, which you will work through later. After recording a memo, continue with the line-by-line or paragraph-by-paragraph analysis.

9 When interpreting a text, you should make comparisons constantly, asking yourself 'What does the first half of the page tell us? Which phenomena are mentioned here? Just how do they work? What could provide an alternative?'

10 As the analysis progresses, the codes become more and more definitive and tend to lose the temporary character that is typical for the open coding phase. This implies that codes are renamed, deleted, summarized, consolidated under one higher-ranking concept, etc.

11 Axial coding begins in the intermediate and advanced stages of the analysis process. Here, individual codes become the focus of the analysis.

Based on the questions listed under 4) above, which should be posed systematically when looking at the material, Strauss schematized the following Coding Paradigm (Flick, 2006, p. 301):

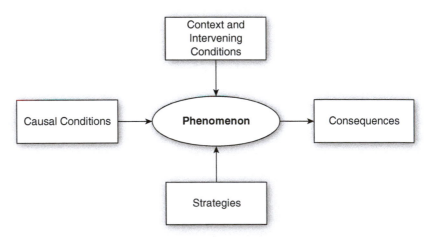

Figure 2.4 The Coding Paradigm

12 Theory building advances with every step of the analysis. The analytical work is arranged in such a way that key categories are extracted throughout the analysis, and the theory is constructed around them. It is possible that one of the axial categories will serve as the decisive key category. If so, it will serve as the foundation for your research report, which should also include your memos, etc.

To summarize, Grounded Theory offers valuable procedures and techniques for working with codes and categories. First and foremost, categorization is granted great importance within the theory. Second, in practice, Grounded Theory also demonstrates that categories can be more or less abstract, and can vary in the degree of generalization and their potential for developing (new) theories. Third, the work with categories in the analysis process is continuous, as you must constantly differentiate between categories, give them dimensions, etc. Finally, the analysis style of Grounded Theory shows quite clearly that there are indeed research concepts that go beyond the simple concept of 'indicator → category → statistical analysis'.

2.3 Content Analysis and Qualitative Content Analysis

In many respects, Max Weber's suggestion at the first German Sociological Association Conference in 1910 that an 'enquiry be conducted of the content of newspapers' marks the birth of content analysis as a method of social science research.

> To be clear, we will have to start simply by using a compass and scissors to measure how newspaper content has shifted quantitatively over the past generation, not only in the advertisement section, but the feuilleton and main articles, even the editorials – everything that is presented as news but no longer is (...). Such studies are only in their beginnings – and from these beginnings, we will move on to qualitative analyses. (Weber, 1911, p. 52)

Weber's suggestion included four aspects that were quite characteristic for the subsequent development of content analysis, including:

- First, content analysis references some form of media – Weber analysed newspapers, while radio, television, and other forms of mass media communications were included in later analyses over the history of content analysis, particularly in the golden age of content analysis in the 1930s (see Krippendorff, 2004, p. 3; Schreier, 2012, pp. 9–13).
- Second, thematic analysis was and still is prototypical of classical content analysis, particularly in the form of frequency analyses of mass media themes. Textbooks

(such as Frueh, 2004) and text collections on content analysis often use this kind of analyses as practical examples.

- Third, quantitative argumentation is central to traditional content analysis – Weber even wanted to cut out newspaper articles and measure their size, while we look at the size of files in bytes today as an indicator of the relevance that a given topic has.
- Fourth, quantitative analysis can be thought of as the beginning, the first step of analysis. More important are qualitative analyses that follow after one has obtained a quantitative overview. Quantitative analysis should therefore not be considered superior to or as a replacement for qualitative analysis.

What makes classical content analysis so interesting for the development of methods for systematic qualitative text analysis is that it is based on nearly one hundred years of experience systematically analysing texts, even a large quantity of texts. This means that it has already encountered (and often solved) a variety of problems that arise when analysing written texts or verbal data, which, in fact is qualitative data.

History of Classical Content Analysis

Scholars like Krippendorff and Merten note that the history of content analysis began a long time ago. Merten sees precursors of content analysis in the exegesis of the Bible or in Sigmund Freud's interpretation of dreams. Within this context, Merten mentions an 'Intuitive Phase', which extends to approximately 1900 (Merten, 1995, pp. 35–36). The actual beginning of scientific content analysis is dated around the beginning of the 20th century and marked by Max Weber's speech at the first German Sociological Association Conference, and his proposal for an 'enquiry of the newspapers', as noted above. Numerous studies and analyses were completed in the field of communications in this 'Descriptive Phase'. The golden age of content analysis came with the invention of the radio and particularly with the analysis of the impact of reporting on the war during the 1940s. Famous projects, such as the 'World Attention Survey' in 1941 and Lasswell's study of war reports and propaganda ('Experimental Division for the Study of Wartime Communication', sponsored by the US government and the Hoover Institute), make it evident that content analysis in the field of communications was also politically important at the time. Under the leadership of Lazarsfeld and in co-operation with Adorno, the Rockefeller Foundation's outstanding 'Radio Project' researched the effects of the mass communication ('propaganda analysis').

The term 'content analysis' was first used in 1940 and many other terms that are central to content analysis, such as 'sampling unit', 'category', and 'intercoder reliability', stem from that time and were coined by leading content analysts like Lasswell, Berelson, and Lazarsfeld. Methodically, content analysis made considerable progress: Berelson wrote the first dissertation using methods of content analysis in 1941 and co-authored the textbook *The Analysis of Communication Content* with Lazarsfeld (1948). In addition, numerous publications and conferences made it possible for researchers to exchange their ideas and methodologies (see Frueh, 2004, pp. 11–15).

Since the end of the 1940s, content analysis has taken on more of a quantifying and statistical character. This must be viewed within the context of a general shift in the social sciences towards behaviourism after the Second World War and into the 1950s and the early 1960s. Empirical research focused on testing hypotheses and theories. Qualitative research was considered unscientific and more and more qualitative elements disappeared from content analysis, which was then limited to the quantitative analysis of the manifest content of communication. Thus, Berelson defined content analysis as follows:

> Content analysis is a research technique for the objective, systematic and quantitative description of the manifest content of communication. (Berelson, 1952, p. 18)

Critique of such a methodically narrow form of content analysis came up early on in 1952. Kracauer, for example, criticized Berelson's content analysis of being too superficial and not grasping the more subtle meanings.

Qualitative Content Analysis

Kracauer was the first to call explicitly for a 'qualitative content analysis' (Kracauer, 1952). Such a qualitative form of content analysis should also address the latent meanings, not in terms of the objective meaning or probable and improbable interpretations, but the latent meaning which you can communicate intersubjectively. Thus, this poses a general question regarding how to interpret texts, which should take the hermeneutics of the classical theory of interpretation into account (see Klafki, 2001, pp. 126–127). From the beginning, the new kind of content analysis – 'qualitative content analysis' – that Kracauer suggested, was different from mainstream content analysis. No longer limited to the manifest content as it was under the dominant behaviourist paradigm, qualitative content analysis focused on discovering the *meaning* within texts and analysing their communicative content (see Kracauer, 1952). Today's qualitative content analysis, as it is practised in German sociology and psychology, is based on these historical precursors, such as the one by Kracauer, that are not limited to the manifest text content or its quantification. In addition, today's approaches rely on hermeneutical traditions, which provide some basic principles for understanding and interpreting texts.

It should be noted that content analysis is often misunderstood to be a method of data *collection*. In fact, it is often described as such in textbooks on research methods even though the term 'content analysis' clearly indicates that it is a method of *analysis*. In addition, unlike surveys, observations, or experiments, content analysis is often characterized as a 'non-reactive method' in which the researchers do not have an influence on the participants. These characterizations are a bit confusing; however, they have developed over time because content analysis, as presented above, has its roots in communication science and media analysis. There, the focus was on analysing existing newspaper and magazine articles or radio broadcasts. These sorts of content analyses are indeed non-reactive because they do not affect the analysed communicative content. However, content analysis is not limited to the analysis of existing data that stems from mass media; rather, it also includes data that researchers gather themselves, such as interviews or observation protocols. In such cases, the analyses can no longer be considered 'non-reactive'. In general, content analyses within the social sciences should be considered as a method of analysis, and not as a method of data collection.

From Kracauer to new conceptualizations of qualitative content analysis

Kracauer conceptualized qualitative content analysis as more of a necessary extension to classical content analysis rather than an alternative form of content analysis. Leading content analysts of that time had argued that different kinds of texts are situated on a continuum. Statements that do not require additional interpretation, such as facts or alleged facts, are situated at one end of the continuum while texts that require interpretation are situated at the other end. For example, the news of a train accident would be on the factual end of the continuum while an example of modern poetry would be at the other end. Kracauer argued, however, that in social science analyses, events such as train accidents that do not require additional interpretation are very rare. In such cases, counting and statistical analysis are indeed appropriate and useful. But even beyond the interpretation of modern poetry, text analysis is not possible without subjective understanding and interpretation of text. The crucial point is that quantitative approaches are not as precise as interpretive approaches when it comes to understanding communication. This can be seen, for example, if the attempt is made to rate a complex communication on a scale with only three points from 'very favourable' to 'very unfavourable' (Kracauer, 1952, p. 631).

Kracauer praised qualitative content analysis as a necessary extension of and supplement to mainstream content analysis, which was becoming more and more quantitative this time. He concluded that a new kind, a *qualitative content analysis* had to be established. In the following decades, more and more researchers who analysed qualitative data in their research started putting Kracauer's ideas of qualitative content analysis into practice. Thus, different approaches to qualitative content analysis developed methodically over time, though they were not specifically considered methods of qualitative content analysis at the time. In 1983, approximately three decades later, Philipp Mayring (2000, 2010), a German psychologist, published his book, *Qualitative Content Analysis*, which became the first methods textbook published about qualitative content analysis.

It was Mayring who started using the term 'qualitative content analysis' again in the 1980s when he ambitiously attempted to develop a contemporary qualitative form of content analysis that drew on different sources from different disciplines and approaches to text analysis (Mayring, 2010). He describes five such sources: a) communication science (content analysis); b) hermeneutics; c) qualitative social research (interpretive paradigm); d) literature and literary studies (systematic text analysis); and e) psychology of processing texts (Mayring, 2010, pp. 26–47).

Mayring has his roots in psychology, a discipline in which content analysis is rare, and even when it is used, it is usually only in a strictly quantitative form. Mayring's approach draws on five different disciplines (see above) and is in many ways similar to classical content analysis paired with qualitative and hermeneutical elements; thus, it is clearly in the tradition of Kracauer (Mayring, 2000, 2010; Schreier, 2012).

To sum it up: Qualitative text analysis is a form of analysis in which an understanding and interpretation of the text play a far larger role than in classical content analysis, which is more limited to the so-called 'manifest content'. Various scholars, such as Frueh and Krippendorff, note that classical content analysis and qualitative content analysis do not diametrically oppose each other; the differences between the two are not that great (see Frueh, 2004, p. 68; Krippendorff, 2004). However, this is not true for many of the examples that these scholars present, such as Frueh's analysis of thematic frequencies, for this kind of quantitative content analysis is indeed quite different from qualitative content analysis since its focus is on counting and subsequent statistical analysis. Still less are the similarities between qualitative analysis and the kind of quantitative content analysis that has been developing in the United States since the middle of the 1960s, which is centered on computer-assisted statistical analysis. In this new mainstream quantitative content analysis, texts are coded automatically using a dictionary, whereby the ambiguity and importance of the words is largely ignored. In contrast, qualitative content analysis presents an interpretive form of analysis in which the codings are completed based on interpretation, classification, and analysis. Moreover, text analysis and coding are not done exclusively by computer, so they are linked to human understanding and interpretation.

2.4 Other Practical Approaches to Qualitative Text Analysis

Descriptions of qualitative text analysis procedures can be found in numerous textbooks and practical research work. Most of these descriptions refer to the analysis of interviews (Lamnek, 2005; Rasmussen, Østergaard, & Beckmann, 2006; Ritchie, Spencer, & O´Connor, 2003). Lamnek (2005, pp. 402–407) describes four phases of the analytic process:

1 Transcription
2 Individual case analysis
3 General analysis
4 Control phase

According to Lamnek, the goal of the individual case analysis is to compile and condense the data by highlighting important passages and eliminating insignificant information. The result is a highly abridged text of the individual interviews that shows the distinctiveness of each, which will be 'integrated and used to characterize the respective interviews' (ibid., p. 404).

> The individual case analysis produces a characteristic of the respective interview that corresponds to the specific passages of the interview or a summary of the respondent's answers that includes the researcher's assessments and comments and is based on distinctive features of the interview. (Lamnek, 2005, p. 404)

The next phase, the *general analysis*, goes beyond the individual interviews to reach more general and theoretical conclusions. Lamnek describes the following steps within the general analysis (see Lamnek, 2005, p. 404):

1 Search for similarities among all or some of the interviews. This can be a step towards a type-building generalization of the interviews.
2 Determine differences in content of the interviews.
3 Examine the similarities and differences to determine general tendencies or syndromes that may be typical for all or some of the respondents.
4 Present and interpret the various types of respondents, statements, information, etc. with reference to the individual cases.

Lamnek explains that you should always design your analysis specifically for a given research question. The methods of data collection and analysis you choose should be developed based on the research question. Thus, the goal is not to conduct your analysis based on fixed methods; rather, you should always keep the research question in mind.

Another approach is formulated by Hopf and Schmidt in course of a social psychology-oriented project on authoritarianism and right-winged extremism (Hopf, Rieker, Sanden-Marcus, & Schmidt, 1995). Here, the analysis process includes the following steps (after the transcription):

Step 1: Develop Categories Based on the Empirical Data

This step involves an intensive examination of the data, including reading through the transcripts multiple times, if necessary. Your own prior knowledge and the research question should direct your attention as you work through the text: Which topics and aspects are addressed? Write your comments next to the text and make note of important terms or concepts. The goal of Step 1 is to understand the respondents' statements.

Step 2: Create a Guideline for Your Analysis

Define the categories that you developed in Step 1 and summarize them to create a guideline for your analysis. If necessary, modify and expand your categories.

Step 3: Code the Data

Assess the data according to your analysis guidelines and your code-book. Code the data by assigning it to evaluative categories. This step involves reducing the richness of information presented in the cases.

Step 4: Setup Tables and Overviews

Present the results of the coding in the form of tables that include the frequencies with which the evaluative categories appear. Create cross-tabs to present the relationships between two or more categories.

Step 5: In-depth Interpretations of Individual Cases

In some cases and for some research questions, it is helpful to focus on individual transcripts. You can summarize and characterize cases by creating detailed descriptions and interpretations of them. Moreover, you can also develop and test your hypotheses (Schmidt, 2010, pp. 482–484).

Many approaches to qualitative text analysis are outlined in detail in research reports and textbooks on research methods (such as in Bernard & Ryan, 2010; Boyatzis, 1998; Flick, 2006; Gibbs, 2009; Guest, MaxQueen, & Namey, 2012). Huberman and Miles' comprehensive textbook, *Qualitative Data Analysis. An Expanded Sourcebook* (1994), is an excellent source for different analysis methods and techniques.

Summary

In this chapter various procedures and techniques for the analysis of textual data have been presented. These are like building blocks for the development of a systematic qualitative text analysis. The objective is to develop a method that combines the strengths of these approaches; a method, which is rule-guided and intersubjective but also interpretive and creative at the same time.

So, what are the key elements of qualitative text analysis? What distinguishes it from other forms of qualitative data analysis? We would like to emphasize the following six points regarding qualitative text analysis:

1 It is the categories, the code-book and the process of coding that are central to the analysis.
2 It is a systematic approach that includes a set of clear rules for each of the individual steps of the analysis.
3 It involves classifying and categorizing all texts of the entire data set and not only selected parts of the data.
4 It uses techniques to create categories based on the data.
5 It involves hermeneutic interpretation and reflection and is aware of the interactive form of the origin of the material.
6 It recognizes quality standards and aims for intercoder agreement.

3

Basic Concepts and the Process of Qualitative Text Analysis

In this chapter, you will learn about:

- The basic terms and main concepts associated with qualitative text analysis.
- The first steps of the analysis process, beginning with a careful reading of each individual text.
- How to work through the text hermeneutically.
- The general sequence of analytic stages in qualitative text analysis.
- How to use memos as useful resources for documenting your own ideas as well as noting anything important or unusual in the texts.
- Why categories and the category system are central to systematic text analysis.
- How to create categories inductively, deductively, and using a mix of the two.
- How to create individual case summaries.

3.1 Main Concepts within Qualitative Text Analysis

In this chapter, we will examine some of the main concepts associated with qualitative text analysis in more detail. As Berelson, one of the founding fathers of classical content analysis, noted:

> Content analysis stands or falls by its categories (...) since the categories contain the substance of the investigation, a content analysis can be no better than its system of categories. (Berelson, 1952, p. 147)

The central role of categories and codes is characteristic not only for classical content analysis, but also for Grounded Theory, thematic analysis, discourse analysis, and other kinds of methods. It is also the core concept of the methods of qualitative text analysis presented in this book. Thus, an explanation of the most important concepts within qualitative text analysis should begin with the term 'category'.

Category

The term 'category' stems from the Greek word κατηγορία (kategoriai), which originally meant class, charge, or even accusation and can be found in many different scientific disciplines, from philosophy and the social sciences to biology, linguistics, and mathematics. Within the context of the social sciences, the term 'category' is usually used in the sense of 'class', i.e. a category is the result of some sort of classification. The classified entities could include people, ideas, institutions, processes, discourses, objects, arguments, and much more. We are familiar with the term 'category' within the context of knowledge systems, such as those presented in encyclopaedias, indexes, or even taxonomy charts. In Wikipedia, the term category is defined as 'a group, often named or numbered, to which items are assigned based on similarity or defined criteria'.[1] It is also helpful to look at synonyms of the word category, which include: class, family, genus, group, and type. Other common synonyms are department, area, rubric, assignment, classification, and kind.

Building categories is a fundamental part of any mental activity. It is a basic cognitive process and, as such, it is the subject of both developmental psychology and epistemological thought. We need such processes of category building to perceive the world around us and organize what we perceive, e.g. to form concepts, make comparisons, and decide which class we should assign a given observation or event to. Such fundamental cognitive processes are necessary for everyday life and decisions as well as for practising science because objects in the world around us do not dictate to which category or class they should be assigned. Thus, we have to assign objects and ideas to categories, and our perceptions and thought processes influence every categorization we make.

Frueh emphasizes the classifying character of categories within the context of content analysis:

> The pragmatic aim of every content analysis is ultimately to reduce complexity while adhering to a certain research-based perspective. Passages of texts are described and classified according to theoretically interesting characteristics.

---

[1]See www.wikipedia.org (accessed 2 May 2011).

By reducing the complexity, some information is lost. First, some of the conversational characteristics of the original text are disregarded because they are not relevant to the given research question. Then, more information is lost when the conversational characteristics are classified. According to specific criteria, some of the characteristics may be examined and deemed similar to each other; thus, they are assigned to a given class or type, which is referred to as a 'category' in content analysis. (2004, p. 42)

The question of what exactly a category represents in empirical research is hardly addressed in literature on research methods, even in textbooks that focus on methods of qualitative data analysis. It is more or less assumed that people already know what a category is, based on common sense. Instead of a definition, you often find a collection of category attributes, particularly in textbooks about qualitative data analysis. There it can be read, for example, that categories should be 'rich', 'meaningful', 'distinguishable' or 'disjunctive'.

Frueh distinguishes between everyday categories and those used within the framework of scientific analysis. Noting that a category is something that

Table 3.1 Different Kinds of Categories Found in the Social Science Literature

Category	Origin (Source)
1201 social aspects > social security.	Category in a classical quantitative content analysis (1201 is the numerical shortcut).
A good relationship with students is definitely possible.	Category as developed in a summarizing qualitative content analysis.
Body-equipment connection.	Category as developed by Anselm Strauss in a Grounded Theory study.
Level at which people are personally affected by climate change: (1) highly affected, (2) moderately affected, (3) not affected, (4) could not be determined.	Evaluative category developed in a study on environmental awareness.
Baker.	Category for classifying occupations.
White-collar crime.	Category for assessing economic fields (quantitative content analysis).
01310 Kosovo conflict.	Thematic category used in a quantitative content analysis in political sciences.
Length of a newspaper article.	Formal category within a media analysis.
Avoiding disclosure.	Category in a Grounded Theory study.
Managing emotions.	Category in a Grounded Theory study.
Potential barriers.	Category used in a youth study.

should be defined clearly, he devises an operational (functional) definition of a category:

> Proper names, for example, do not require a categorical definition because they do not need to be classified or differentiated. If multiple proper names are compiled to form a category, a simple count of how many names there are in the category would suffice as a definition. This, however, is not as obvious for a word like 'structure'. Is the meaning of the word completely clear or does it require clarification? The answer becomes quite clear if you consider the following list of words associated with structure: *house, column, stadium, tent, garden wall, bridge, walkway, playground,* (…). The fact that all of these terms could undoubtedly be considered structures (using the simple criterion that they were built) shows that even such a simple and superficially clear category such as 'structure' must be defined, particularly if a researcher might wish to exclude some of the associated words in order to focus on his or her research interest. (Frueh, 2004, p. 40)[2]

The list of examples from social science literature in Table 3.1 illustrates just how diverse the spectrum of what is considered a category is in the social sciences.

It is obvious, then, that the spectrum of what is considered a category is quite broad. We can differentiate between (at least) five different kinds of categories:

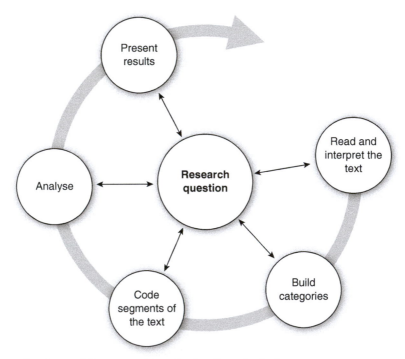

Figure 3.1   General Process of Qualitative Text Analysis

---

[2]Translated from German.

a) Factual categories

These are categories that refer to certain objective or seemingly objective occurrences, such as to classify different occupations (someone is a 'politician', another person says, 'I am a baker') or to refer to a specific place ('I live in Springfield'; 'I live in a redeveloped area').

b) Thematic categories

Here, a category refers to a specific content, such as a topic, a specific argument, a person, etc. In most cases within qualitative text analysis, categories refer to topics, such as 'political involvement', 'consumer behaviour', or 'knowledge of the environment'. Different passages within an interview that contain information pertaining to the category are then marked accordingly.

c) Evaluative categories

These categories have a defined number of characteristics and levels that are used to assess the information in the text. For example, the category 'helper syndrome' may be characterized as 'strong', 'little', or 'none'. Coders would examine appropriate text passages, rate the level, and assign the appropriate characteristic.

d) Formal categories

This type of category refers to dates and information about the analysis unit itself. For an open interview, for example, this would be the length of the interview in minutes, the date of the interview, the name of the interviewer, and the length of the transcription in bytes.

e) Analytical or theoretical categories

These categories are results of the work of the analysts – they are not descriptive but part of a deeper analysis. Analytical categories cannot always be clearly distinguished from thematic and evaluative categories. In the beginning of the analysis you may identify themes like 'use of energy', 'consumption of organic food' in an interview and define categories that are near to the language of your respondents. These are typical descriptive categories. In the later stages of the analysis you may integrate these categories to 'environmental behaviour' which is definitely an analytical category.

When students are reading textbooks on social research methods, they are often surprised to find that the term category is used so diversely. While in one case a category may appear like a variable in quantitative analysis, with different characteristics ('Level at which people are personally affected by climate change'), it is more like a statement in another case ('Whatever the case, we can achieve a good relationship with students'). The distinction between the term 'category' and other terms such as concept, variable, and code is often quite unclear.

Concept

The term concept is often used as an alternative to the term category. Concepts are, according to Schnell et al. (2008), structuring terms, such as power, identity, and integration. Concepts lead to constructs, but do not present any clear direction that can be measured. 'Ethnic identity' is an example of a concept presented by Schnell et al. Using a dimensional analysis you may specify what aspects of a subject are referred to by a given concept (Schnell et al., 2008, pp. 127–133). In the example above, the individual elements of the concept 'Ethnic identity', 'ethnicity' and 'identity', must be presented separately and defined as precisely as possible.

Variable

The term variable is also considered an alternative to category. A variable is a feature that varies according to the object under examination (constants, in contrast, are features shared by all of the objects that are being examined, e.g. all of the students at a school for girls are female). A variable has at least two characteristics, which are also referred to as variable values. In empirical social research, the term 'variable' always refers to a measured or potentially measurable characteristic: While 'variable' is clearly associated with a quantitative research style, 'concept' is equally suited for both quantitative and qualitative approaches because of its strongly theoretical nature.

Code

The term 'code', as Bernard and Ryan (2010, p. 87) pointed out, has three different meanings:

a) Code as an encryption device. Names and locations are coded to hide information.
b) Code as a tool for tagging and indexing a text.
c) Code as a value code to indicate the amount of a particular characteristic.

In qualitative data analysis, codes are used especially in Grounded Theory, in which the terms code and coding appear in several different forms, including open codes, axial codes, and selective codes as well as in combination with other elements, such as substantive codes, key codes, and theoretical codes (see Strauss & Corbin, 1996, p. 43 ff.). The term code was originally used in quantitative research approaches; in Grounded Theory, coding refers to analysing, naming, categorizing, and theoretically organizing the data, which is in the sense of the second point mentioned by Bernard and Ryan. Thus, because of the different tasks associated with the different phases of the analysis process, codes are sometimes referred to as categories; other times, they represent initial, ad-hoc concepts that may be further developed into categories later in the analysis process.

You may be asking yourself why it is necessary to construct such vague distinctions for their use when all of the terms seem so similar, particularly because the term code seems to have the same meaning as the term concept. In fact, some methods textbooks and research approaches do consider the terms to refer to the same thing. In Grounded Theory textbooks, for example, there is often no effort to make a clear distinction between a category and a code. The following sections of this book work with the pragmatic definitions described above and refer to a category as the result of a classification of different units.

At this point, it should be sufficient to note that categories are concepts that have a relatively high degree of complexity. In this sense, 'structure', 'force', ' 'core energy', 'renewable energy', and 'politicians' as well as 'war-like conflict', 'knowledge of the environment', 'learning style', 'sense of responsibility', and 'study strategy' are considered categories. These concepts can only be adopted as categories within content analysis once they have been defined more precisely. To define a category, you must describe its content and determine indicators that should help coders assign the categories consistently and confidently. While your list of indicators as well as your examples that stem from the interview transcripts may never be complete, they nevertheless provide guidelines for assigning the categories. Thus, the definition of a category is located somewhere between a nominal definition[3] and an operational (functional) definition. In some forms of traditional content analysis, such as a dictionary-based content analysis, categories are defined operationally as lists of words that effect the coding of a category whenever a word of the list appears, for instance the words 'pension' or 'unemployment benefits' would mean that the category 'social system' would therefore be coded.

---

[3]For an overview of different definitions, see Schnell et al., 2008, pp. 50–53.

Segments

As mentioned above, a category is the result of some kind of classification. In qualitative text analysis categories are always linked to text or parts of a text like words, sentences, paragraphs or even pages or chapters. These parts of a text are usually named 'segments', 'chunks', or 'quotations'. In general, the process of coding text may have two directions: from text to code(s) or from code(s) to text. The first way means to create new codes when working through a text. This is a creative act and of course two scholars or coders will rarely define exactly the same codes. The alternative way goes the opposite way: a code or category already exists and a part of a text is identified as an instance of this particular code and is coded. The result of both is the same – connections between a code and pieces of text.

The smallest unit that can be assigned to a category is a single word, as it is not very useful to code individual characters or symbols. There are two ways to examine a text: You can start with an a-priori given category, examine the text, and assign the code to every segment of text where the particular theme is mentioned. You may also work in the other direction by reading the text, identifying recurrent themes, defining appropriate codes and associating the text passages with them. This second approach is especially useful for developing new concepts and categories. Either way, there is a clear connection between the text passages and categories.

Units

Another fundamental term stemming from classical content analysis is the term 'unit', which appears there in different combinations, including sampling unit, recording unit, analysis unit, content unit, and context unit. These terms do not have uniform meanings in the literature about methods and techniques within content analysis and qualitative text analysis. Thus, the following explanation, based on definitions by Krippendorff (2004) and Roessler (2005), should clarify the terms and concepts.

Sampling units: These are the basic unit of analysis and are selected from the data (that is, all of the objects to potentially be examined) for the content analysis using specific selection methods (such as random selections, quota selections, or arbitrary selections; see Diekmann, 2007, pp. 373–398; Flick, 2006, pp. 122–141). A sampling unit could be a specific edition of a newspaper, an open-ended interview, a narrative interview, a children's book, a parliamentary speech, etc. In many respects, sampling units represent physical units. If, for example, you would like to examine the portrayal of grandparents in children's books for preschoolers, each individual book would be considered a sampling unit.

Recording units: While sampling units are concerned with what units should be included or excluded from a given study, recording units address the way in which data is included in a traditional content analysis. Krippendorff defined recording units as follows:

> [Recording units] are units that are distinguished for separate description, transcription, recording or coding. (Krippendorff, 2004, p. 99)

In principle, one sampling unit can contain multiple recording units. If you are analysing media, such as the way in which a political conflict was reported in a daily newspaper, it would make sense to select the individual articles as recording units. The sampling unit (the edition of the given newspaper on a given day) would contain multiple recording units (articles). Recording units are always a part of the sampling unit and never extend beyond it; sometimes they can be considered one and the same, such as in the case of a transcript of a qualitative interview, which does not contain any further sub-units.

Content units: In classical quantitative content analysis, a unit of coding refers to a single feature that determines how a word or concept should be coded, i.e. assigned to a category. For example, the words and names 'Bill Clinton', 'Barack Obama', 'George W. Bush', 'Bush Senior', etc. would be assigned to the category 'president of the United States'. According to Krippendorff, content units can be determined formally or based on content: Formal factors for determining content units include the length and breadth of the data as well as the date on which it was collected. Moreover, content units can be referential (referring to specific people, places, etc.), propositional (referring to specific statements or judgements), or thematic (referring to specific topics or discourses). In classical content analysis, a content unit should only fit one category. For example, 'Bill Clinton' would only serve as an indicator for the category 'president of the United States' and not the category 'lawyer'.

In qualitative text analysis, usually the terms *text segment* or *coded segment* are used instead of content unit. The bi-directional nature of this approach is what makes qualitative text analysis different from classical content analysis: In classical content analysis, codings are completed on a higher analytical level (numerical data as part of a data matrix) so that it is no longer necessary to refer back to the original data after this step of the analysis. In qualitative text analysis, the categories stay connected to the data throughout the entire analysis process and it is often quite useful to refer back to the original text.

Context units: The term context unit is related to the work of the analysts (coders). A context unit is defined as the largest unit that needs to be included in the analysis in order to correctly record and categorize text passages.

Normally, a context unit is no larger than the given recording unit; however, there are exceptions to this rule, such as in qualitative panel studies in which multiple interviews are carried out with participants and it is possible to refer back to other interviews that were carried out with the same individuals.

This marks a difference to hermeneutics where the context that may be included into the analysis is not limited. For instance, imagine the question of how to interpret a politician's statement – the greater the political knowledge of the scholar, the wider the context that is taken into account. So context in hermeneutics is a question of the knowledge of the interpreter and not a question of formally fixed limits.

Unlike as in classical content analysis, qualitative text analysis does not work with pre-fixed units. In classical content analysis a text is first segmented into units and these units are then coded usually only with one single code. In qualitative text analysis the analysis process is different regardless of whether you go from text to codes or from codes to text: segments emerge in the process of coding. You may compare this to the process of marking passages of a book using a highlighter. You mark a semantic unit and write a term or comment in the margin, you are not forced to mark only whole paragraphs or any kind of pre-fixed text unit.

Coders and Intercoder Agreement

A coder is a person who assigns categories to the data, more specifically, to the different text passages within the qualitative data. Each assignment is referred to as a coding. Often, particularly when there is a large amount of text to be processed and coded, the research team pulls in additional personnel to take care of coding the data. In qualitative data analysis, coders must demonstrate an adequate level of competence in interpreting the data, which means they must be well informed about the research question, the theoretical constructions, and the meanings of the categories. To this end, coders are trained prior to beginning the actual codings. Such trainings continue until the coders reach a given level of agreement in their codings (so called 'intercoder agreement'). In classical content analysis, appropriate coefficients were calculated in order to determine the so-called intercoder reliability or interrater reliability, including Krippendorff's Alpha, Cohen's Kappa, Scott's Pi, and others (Krippendorff, 2004, pp. 244–256). In contrast, qualitative text analysis tends to use a procedural approach that aims at minimizing coding differences by discussing and resolving any questionable or conflicting codings as a research team. This approach has been referred to as 'consensual coding' (see Hopf & Schmidt, 1993, pp. 61–63). Generally speaking, one key difference between qualitative text analysis and classical content analysis research practice can be found in the role of the coders: While quantitative content analysis usually relies on personnel that have been trained specifically for this task, members of the research team or the researchers themselves usually complete the coding in qualitative text analysis.

If multiple coders are used in qualitative text analysis, you must check for intercoder agreement. This does not mean that you have to calculate interrater-reliability coefficients, but you must use appropriate procedures, such as 'consensual coding', to ensure that the coders agree in their understanding of how to apply the category system.

3.2 Analysis Processes in Qualitative Text Analysis and Classical Content Analysis

Classical content analysis sticks to a relatively strict model of phases. While different textbooks present different models, they are quite similar. The classical process includes the following five phases:

1 *Planning phase* – Researchers formulate the research question, or even develop hypotheses based on existing theories relating to the subject at hand, and define the selection methods and other methods to be used. They should also compile a sample of analytical units.
2 *Development phase* – This phase centres on developing a category system and defining categories. Researchers must also formulate rules for coding so that the categories can be suitably assigned to text passages and coding units.
3 *Test phase (sample coding)* – The research team's coders are trained and their intercoder reliability is calculated to ensure that they agree. The category system should be tested on a sample of the data and modified or improved, if necessary. Training should continue until sufficient reliability is achieved.
4 *Coding phase* – The data set is randomly assigned to coders, who code it in its entirety.
5 *Analysis phase* – The data matrix produced in the fourth phase is analysed statistically.

The sequence *research question* → *data collection* → *data analysis* is rather characteristic for all forms of empirical research; thus, it can be found in classical content analysis as well as in different kinds of qualitative data analysis. However, qualitative text analysis always includes additional steps for iterations and feedback. The following diagram (Figure 3.1) portrays this sequential process and highlights its circular nature. Unlike in the classical model, the analysis process should be seen as a non-linear process in which the different phases – or method areas – are not strictly separated from each other. It is even possible to acquire additional data after the category system has been established and the majority of the data has been coded. The diagram, which contains five method areas, illustrates that the research question plays a different role in qualitative text analysis: It is posed at the beginning of the research process, but it does not remain unchanged as in the classical hypothetical-deductive model only to be answered at the end of the analysis. Instead, the research question is central to each of the five method areas and can be changed dynamically during the analysis process (within certain constraints). For example, you may wish to make the research question more precise, place new aspects in the forefront, or modify the research question because of unexpected discoveries.

At first glance, the analysis processes of qualitative text analysis and quantitative content analysis might seem quite similar; however, considerable differences between the two become more apparent once you take a closer look. Qualitative text analysis does not have to be guided by specific theories from the beginning. Moreover, working through the text introduces the analysis and is part of every phase of the analysis process. Even more differences between qualitative and quantitative analysis become obvious in research practice. Thus, despite their formal similarities, qualitative text analysis is different from classical content analysis in many ways:

- It is not necessary to formulate hypothesis at the beginning of the planning phase. In fact, it is rarely a part of qualitative text analysis.
- The different phases of qualitative text analysis are not separated from each other as strictly as they are in analysis models based on the classical hypothetico-deductive model. Instead, you can analyse some data while still acquiring other data. Feedback cycles and iterations are also common. In the following chapter, the term phase is used instead of step to indicate that the process is not comprised of fixed steps. At the same time, qualitative text analysis follows a progression that is characteristic in all research settings from formulating the research question to the analysis and finally to the reporting of results.
- The data is coded in its context – neither automatically nor focused only on small units, but rather hermeneutically and interpretively.
- The original data, i.e. the verbal data, maintain their importance even after the coding process. They are not 'finished' after the coding process, nor are they superfluous to the remainder of the analysis.

- In the different kinds of qualitative text analysis, the categories have more of a structuring and systematizing role and do not simply serve to transfer the empirical data into a number or relation.
- The analysis of the coded data is not necessarily a statistical analysis. While statistical analyses can be part of qualitative text analysis, they may only play a minor role. Or, you can even choose to omit statistical analyses completely.

The phases centred on developing and modifying categories in which researchers progressively work with the data are very important phases of the analysis process. Even if qualitative analysis is based on specific theories and hypotheses are formed – which is not out of the question – you can fine-tune the categories during the analysis process and add new categories if you deem it necessary while working through the data. You can even construct new evaluative categories or assign types after analysing the thematic categories, both of which would require you to recode the data.

Like in classical content analysis, working with categories and the subsequent category-based analysis are central to qualitative text analysis. Thus, it is important to take a closer look at how the categories are actually developed.

3.3 Starting a Qualitative Text Analysis: Initial Work with the Text, Memos, and Case Summaries

Before beginning with qualitative text analysis, you should review the goals of your empirical study, asking yourself: What exactly would I like to find out? Which questions am I interested in and what is my focus? Which concepts and constructs are important to my study? What relationships would I like to examine? What sorts of preliminary assumptions do I have regarding these relationships?

Clarifying your objectives in this manner does not violate the principle of openness, which is frequently named as a characteristic of qualitative research. The postulate of openness refers first to the process of data acquisition, as respondents should have the opportunity to express their own views, use their own words instead of being forced to use predetermined categories, and express their individual motives and reasoning. The term 'openness' should not be misunderstood to imply that researchers should 'approach every project without any sort of research question or concept' since we operate on the basis of previous knowledge, assumptions, and world-views that influence every observation we make. Moreover, approaching research too openly would ignore the scientific community, which has already established many research traditions that deal with many different subject matters.

Initial Work with the Text

The first step you take in analysing qualitative data should always be hermeneutical or interpretive in nature and involves reading the text carefully and trying to understand it. It may also be possible to refer back to the actual raw data in the form of audio- and video-recordings.

> We cannot analyse our data unless we read it. How well we read it may determine how well we analyse it. (...) The aim of reading through our data is to prepare the ground for the analysis. (Dey, 1993, p. 83)

This first step is called *initial work with the text* here; in literary studies, working through the text is understood to refer to working through the content and the language of a given text. Starting with the first line, you must read the text sequentially and completely. The goal is to gain a general understanding of the given text on the basis of the research question(s). It is often helpful to outline your research questions and attempt to answer them as you work though the interview data. For example, in a study about individual perception of climate change, we were able to answer or address the following points while reading through each of the interviews:

- What does the respondent actually know about climate change?
- How does he or she relate to it?
- How does he or she personally act or behave?
- Does he or she have any demands or expectations for him or herself?
- Does the respondent discuss the topic with friends or others?

It can also be useful to examine the text formally: How long is the text? Which words are used (particularly noticeable words)? What sort of language does the respondent use? How long are the sentences? What sorts of metaphors are used?

So, what does it mean to systematically read and work through a text? Reading is an everyday skill that we have mastered and we have developed a variety of individual reading techniques within the sciences. Some people highlight texts with one or more multi-coloured highlighters, some people write notes in the margins using their own abbreviations, and others record their notes on other pieces of paper, index cards, or in a research journal. The list of such individual techniques that have proved effective over time is long; such methods should be by no means considered inappropriate here. However, there is a strict procedure that must be followed in qualitative text analysis in order to ensure its comparability, understandability, and methodological control, and it will be explained in more detail in the steps below. Moreover, it should also be noted that many of the tried and true methods mentioned above (highlighting, etc.) can also be used in QDA software programs (see Chapter 6).

In qualitative research, there is not a very strict distinction between the phase of data acquisition and that of data analysis like there is in the classical model of quantitative research. This is also true for qualitative text analysis. Unlike in statistical analyses of standardized data, you do not have to wait to begin analysing the data until all of the data has been collected. Thus, normally you can start analysing the data you have already collected while continuing to collect additional data. Even if you do not adhere to the Grounded Theory, in which data acquisition and analysis are explicitly crossed, it is beneficial to start analysing the content before all of the data has been collected. Hence, you can start reading and working through the first interview as soon as it has been transcribed.

Initial work with the text involves:

- Analysing the text in light of the research question
- Reading the text intently
- Highlighting central terms and concepts
- Marking and making note of important passages
- Marking passages that are difficult to understand
- Analysing arguments and lines of argumentation
- Examining the formal structure (i.e. length, etc.)
- Identifying the internal structure (i.e. paragraphs, breaks, etc.)
- Directing your attention to the general progression of the text.

Working with Memos

Whether you work directly on the computer screen or rely on a printed version of the text depends on your own personal work preferences and style. Many people find it helpful to read through a printed version of the text first so that they can make notes in the margins and highlight passages that seem particularly important. If you choose to do so, make sure that the paragraphs or lines are numbered so that it is easier to transfer your markings and comments into the electronic version later. On the screen, you can highlight important or notable passages using an electronic highlighter.

Any peculiarities in the text or ideas that you may have while reading the text should be recorded as memos.

> A memo contains any thoughts, ideas, assumptions, or hypotheses that occur to researchers during the analysis process. Memos can be short notes (like a Post-it note that you would stick on the page of a book) or more reflective comments regarding the content which act as building blocks for the research report. Writing memos should be considered an integral part of the research process.

Grounded Theory addresses the role that memos play in the research process in detail (see Strauss & Corbin, 1996, pp. 169–192) and differentiates between different types of memos. While memos are not quite as important within the framework of qualitative text analysis as they are in Grounded Theory, they are considered helpful resources that can be used throughout the entire research process, just as they can be in Grounded Theory.

Case Summaries

After working through the text, it is helpful to write a case summary – a systematic, ordered summary of what is characteristic to the given case. A case summary is really just a summarizing case description that focuses on what is important to the research question(s). It should note any characteristics of the individual case that are central to the research question. Unlike memos, case summaries should not contain your own ideas or even hypotheses that you may have developed while working through the text; instead, case summaries are fact-oriented and stay close to the original text.

In our study of individual perception of climate change, described in more detail below, we considered the questions listed above in writing the case summaries: What does the respondent know about climate change? How does he or she relate to it? How does he or she act personally? Does he or she have any demands on or expectations for herself? Does he or she talk with her friends or others about the subject? In addition, case summaries should address two questions that include a comparative aspect: How would you characterize this respondent? What makes this person or this perspective unique?

Case summaries are fact-oriented and based on what was said, not on a hermeneutic or psychological interpretation of the story. Any assumptions made in the text that seem plausible but cannot be confirmed by the information provided in the text should not be noted.

So, what does a case summary look like and how long should it be? For relatively short texts, we recommend simply noting key words. For interviews, it is common to create a title or motto for each of the case summaries. For example, one of my research teams created key word summaries of the cases in a qualitative evaluation project, in which the participants of a university lecture course on statistics were asked about their individual study methods and behaviour as well as their overall experiences in the different sections of the course. Below are two examples from Kuckartz et al.'s evaluation study (2008, pp. 34–35), in which students were asked for their experiences and reviews of a university course on statistics.

Interview with Person R1 – Motto: Positive Attitude without Ambition

She only found the tutoring sessions in the second half of the semester interesting.

The tutoring and practice sessions were the best, but they were too full towards the end.

People attended the tutoring sessions instead of preparing for class and reviewing afterwards on their own.

The basic structure of the lecture seems fine. It inspires productive learning.

She did not have her own study group (rather, she studied with a friend).

She wished she had a small study group.

Did not read any additional material, but finds her own notes good.

The practice test was good and all she wants is to pass the course.

Interview with Person R2 – Motto: The Economical Self-learner

Rarely went to the lectures, but participated in the tutoring sessions more regularly.

Always liked math in school and now likes statistics, too.

Can concentrate better at home, which is why she didn't go to the lectures.

The lectures were useless because she didn't understand anything.

Practice exercises with solutions on the Internet were her source for learning materials.

Bought the recommended textbook and worked through it.

Found the tutoring sessions very good.

Also attended another more practical lecture course on statistics.

Her study methods changed fundamentally in the middle of the course.

She suggests that there be more time to solve practice problems and more material presented in such a way that the students must take their own notes.

Feels like she was well prepared for the final exam.

Case summaries can also take the form of a detailed, fluid text. They can be written not only for individual interviews, but also for qualitative studies with groups and organizations using mottos. A motto can focus on a particular aspect of the research question, be based on a statement or quote in the given text, or be creatively formulated by the researchers to fit a given text. However, because mottos are accentuated characterizations, they are highly subject to interpretation. Thus, while a motto can be useful, it may not always be.

In the analysis process, case summaries should be created for all of the interviews within a given study. They provide an overview of the spectrum of individual cases included in the study, which is particularly valuable in studies with a large number of cases. You can compare and contrast cases that appear particularly similar or particularly different using the criteria of maximum and minimum contrasts.

These kinds of case summaries are meaningful for the research process for four main reasons:

- *First*, they provide an overview of interviews for larger research teams in which not every team member can systematically work through every text (team aspect).
- *Second*, the summaries are a good starting point for creating tabular case overviews for multiple cases (comparative aspect).
- *Third*, they highlight the differences between the individual cases (aspect of analytical differentiation).
- *Fourth*, they help to generate hypotheses and categories.

3.4 Constructing Categories

If you choose to conduct a qualitative data analysis, you will likely ask yourself, 'How do I determine which categories to use?', 'How many categories are necessary?', or 'What rules do I have to follow in constructing the categories?' In literature on research methods, little information is given about how exactly categories are built because it is assumed to follow common sense. You may come across rather unhelpful statements like, 'There are no patent remedies for constructing categories' (Kriz & Lisch, 1988, p. 134). At the same time, the same textbooks point out that category construction is very relevant for the analysis and protagonists argue that content analysis stands or falls with its categories. So, you may be asking yourself, how in the world can you even construct something as important as a category?

The most suitable way to create the categories depends largely on the research question at hand and any previous knowledge that researchers have about the given research subject or field. The more theory-oriented the project, the more extensive the previous knowledge, the more focused the research question, and the more specific the existing hypotheses, the easier it is to create categories while reading through the collected data. Generally speaking, theoretical and empirical methods for constructing categories are situated at opposite poles on a spectrum.

Methods for Creating Categories

Theoretical ◄───────────────────────────────► Empirical

Figure 3.2   The Two Poles of Category Construction

Constructing categories based solely on the empirical data is often referred to as *inductive category construction*. One technique for developing inductive categories was described in detail by Mayring and is called 'summarizing content analysis' (see 2010, pp. 67–83). Using this technique, you can construct categories by paraphrasing, generalizing, and abstracting the original data.

Constructing categories based on existing theories about the subject and existing hypotheses is called *deductive category construction*.

Building categories and the processes of identifying and classifying corresponding text passages can be considered both:

a) an act of classification and incorporation; and
b) a creative act, i.e. creating a new term or concept for a class of phenomena that is deemed to be the same.

It is not as contradictory as it may seem to construct categories inductively and deductively and use them in qualitative text analysis. After all, the entire data set is typically coded within qualitative text analysis, which means that all the data is processed systematically based on the category system. When working with a category scheme, the same rules and standards apply, regardless of whether the categories have been developed using the data or without empirical data. In the following, the fundamentals behind inductive and deductive category construction will be described in greater detail. Then, common combinations of the two that are frequently found in research practice and considerations regarding how to implement category systems will be addressed.

Constructing Categories without Empirical Data

Deductive categories are derived from category systems that existed before the empirical data was collected. The term 'deductive' refers to a 'top-down logic':

The categories can stem from theories or hypotheses as well as interview guides and existing systematic arrangements.

The following simple example should help clarify what categories can be considered deductive categories: A well-known newspaper differentiates between the following six rubrics:

1   Politics
2   Business
3   Finance
4   Sport
5   Culture
6   Miscellaneous

The different categories seem plausible because they are based on everyday knowledge and the perceived social realities in our culture, in which these categorical differentiations can be found in disciplines and governmental agencies. Thus, any new story that appears on the news ticker can be 'coded' appropriately and forwarded to the appropriate editor or division, as can be seen in the following table:

Time	Headline	Category Assigned
18:48	Man trapped by avalanche freed by companions	Miscellaneous
18:24	NASDAQ at lowest point since Fall 2004	Finance
17:58	Spectacular jailbreak in Athens	Miscellaneous
17:22	Obama and Putin continue to disagree	Politics
16:17	Another avalanche in the Rockies	Miscellaneous
16:11	GM management to reveal plans for renovations on Friday	Business
15:52	Obama wants to cut the deficit in half	Business
15:16	Vattenfall Power and Gas Co. continues to grow	Business
15:10	*Slumdog Millionaire* wins Best Film at the Oscars	Culture
15:08	Germany is losing more and more residents	Miscellaneous

Figure 3.3   News Headlines Sorted into Pre-Defined Categories

Clearly, some stories or topics are difficult to assign. For example, it is not clear if the story with the headline 'NASDAQ at lowest point since Fall 2004' should be assigned to the 'business' or 'finance' category. Thus, it is imperative to formulate criteria to differentiate between the categories that encompass the intentions behind the classifications so that coders can reliably assign the headlines and code the data.

The largest difficulty in constructing categories deductively lies in precisely formulating category definitions so that they do not overlap. Moreover, the categories must be exhaustive. For example, the category scheme with six categories presented above could hardly be used if we forgot to include a category like 'business'. Also, it is always important to include a category for topics that may not fit any of the other categories ('miscellaneous' here); this will allow you to assign all of the data. Thus, the first requirement of deductive categories is that they are *disjunctive and exhaustive* (see Diekmann, 2007, p. 589; Krippendorff, 2004, pp. 351–352). This is necessary in order to achieve an appropriate standard when implementing the categories. That brings us to the question of quality standards. When implementing categories, the classical standard of reliability applies, i.e. coders should demonstrate a high degree of agreement in their codings. Moreover, working with multiple coders improves the quality of the work and is therefore preferable.

Categories that have been constructed deductively are *applied* to empirical social research data, meaning that they existed before the data was examined and coded. This approach does not have to be considered as connected exclusively to qualitative or quantitative research. In the study on 'Family and Right-winged Extremism', described above, Hopf et al. (1995) use a qualitative study to examine the extent to which attachment theories explain the existence of right-winged, radical attitudes in teenagers. The analysis categories 'moderately connected', 'very connected', etc. and their definitions stem from the well-known research on attachment. The research process itself, which included multiple biographical interviews, fulfils all of the criteria in qualitative research, such as openness, communicability, etc. (Hopf & Schmidt, 1993).

When using deductive categories, you may discover that the categories are not precise enough or that too much of the data is being classified as 'miscellaneous' or 'other'. This may lead you to modify existing categories or even define new ones. Even if you have developed your categories deductively, it is still possible to make changes to the category scheme (and to the definitions of categories), which means that you may not adhere to the initial definitions.

If tools or methods are used to structure how data is acquired, such as interview guides for open interviews, researchers often choose to derive their main categories directly from the interview guide in the first phase of qualitative text analysis. Thus, they often begin with deductive categories and develop further, inductive categories and sub-categories using the empirical data. This combination of deductive and inductive categories is described in more detail in Chapter 4.3 ('Thematic Qualitative Text Analysis').

When comparing qualitative and quantitative methods for constructing categories, deductive category construction is often associated with quantitative research. This is accurate for research that uses standard instruments and is based on theories. However, quantitative research can also have a descriptive nature and create categories inductively. In explorative factor analysis, there is even a statistical approach that helps quantitative researchers to differentiate between different dimensions and develop and explore categories inductively.

Creating Categories Based on the Data

Constructing categories inductively refers to developing categories directly using the data, meaning that the categories are not derived on the basis of theories or hypotheses or based on a general, thematic structure in the given field. The following scheme, originally presented by Mayring (2010, pp. 83–85), which has been expanded and made more concrete, presents the general processes involved in creating categories:

1   *Determine the goal of building categories based on your research question*

What am I trying to achieve by building categories? There is no generally accepted way to read a text and define categories. All human perception is targeted.

2   *Determine the degree to which you would like to differentiate your categories*

How many main categories seem suitable for the analysis and for the presentation in my planned research report? This doesn't mean that you should determine the exact number of categories – this is of course not possible for any inductive process of category building. But it means you should be aware of the research process as a whole and of the limitations that are given by the goal of the report and the recipients. So, from the beginning of the analysis you have to ask yourself the questions: What would I like the results to communicate? To which degree can I differentiate for my audience and what will be the appropriate balance between differentiation and summarization? The answers to these questions have consequences on the structure and the degree of differentiation of your coding scheme. It doesn't make sense to build a very fine-grained coding scheme when you already know that the subsequent report requires a much higher level of summarization and generalization.

3   *Set level of abstraction*

How closely do I intend to stick to how participants formulated their statements? How much do I intend to work with abstract categories? Example: A participant describes her actions in separating trash. Should I define the category 'separating trash' or more abstract categories, such as 'individual recycling behaviour' or even more generally, 'individual behaviour towards the environment?'

4   Begin with the first text passage and create a category

The order of the text passages is not really important; however, you should be careful not to get confused when working through the text or even consider making a random or quota selection of the data in some cases.

5   Read the text passage sequentially line-by-line and construct categories directly using the text

For example, highlight and mark the text on paper and write comments in the margins or use a QDA software program to do so electronically by assigning codes to the given text passage. The categories themselves may be comprised of single or combined terms or, such as in the case of argumentation and discourse analyses, of an argument, phrase, or even a short sentence.

6   Assign categories or create additional categories

If a text passage corresponds to an existing category, simply assign it to it. Otherwise, you may need to create a new category. If this new category is similar to one of the categories that you have already defined, you may be able to create a new, more abstract category 'on the fly'.

7   If necessary, rearrange your category system and proceed with the next relevant text passage

Sometimes you will have to take a break and modify your category system: By grouping the categories together, you can combine them to form abstract categories, if appropriate, and maintain the goal of creating the optimal number of categories and the appropriate level of abstraction.

8   Fix the category system

After a while, you will notice that there is no need for additional categories. Thus, the category system can be fixed and you can create a final version of the category guidelines as well as the definitions using suitable examples.

How much data should you process in this way to arrive at an optimal coding scheme? This question cannot be answered so generally, as you will have to work through as many text passages as necessary until you feel that no new aspects are surfacing within the text. Depending on the size and complexity of the data to be analysed, this may be the case after you have processed 10% of

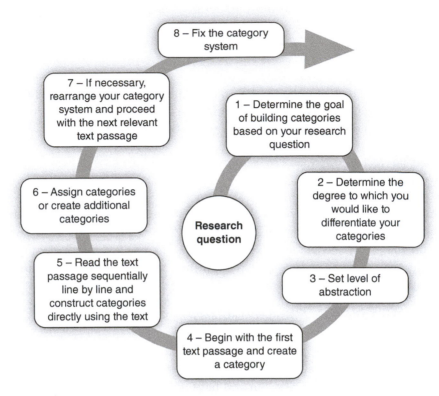

Figure 3.4 The Process of Creating Categories Inductively

the text, or you may have to process 50%. Normally, you will have to process the data in several cycles – some categories can be grouped together according to their similarity, while other categories may have started out too broad and have to be sub-divided.

Although it may seem like inductive categories simply emerge from the data, you should avoid this kind of naïve assumption and keep the aforementioned hermeneutical perspective in mind – that you cannot gain an understanding of the text without solid prior knowledge and understanding.

Constructing Categories Inductively in Grounded Theory

Over its 40-year history, Grounded Theory has addressed how categories should be constructed more intensively than most other methods (see Charmaz & Bryant, 2007; Glaser & Strauss, 1998; Strauss & Corbin, 1996). While coding and constructing categories within Grounded Theory is quite different than in qualitative text analysis, the approach serves as a valuable inspiration for building categories within the framework of qualitative text analysis. Strictly speaking, it should not be referred to as the approach to building categories within *the* Grounded Theory because the theory itself has developed in a variety of different directions.[4] For space reasons, we will not discuss the different directions and alternatives here (Charmaz, 2006, 2011; Kelle, 2007a).

Grounded Theory is a research style that explicitly focuses on generating hypotheses and theories and aims to develop categories directly on the data through a multifaceted process. *Open coding* represents the first step in working through the data. It is centred on identifying and/or naming concepts. In Grounded Theory, concepts are labels or tags for phenomena and they serve as the foundation for generating a given theory. Strauss and Corbin (1996, pp. 43–46) name the following examples of concepts: 'attention', 'transfer information', 'offer support', 'monitor', 'satisfaction of guests', and 'experience'. In Grounded Theory, the entire analysis process is considered to be part of the coding process while 'coding' is used more specifically in qualitative text analysis to refer to the actual assignment of codes (categories) to sections of the data. Concepts have a similar role as in standardized quantitative research. Specifying concepts requires you to step away from the data and work towards developing theories. Strauss and Corbin also refer to coding as diving into the data. You can proceed line-by-line or consider sentences, paragraphs, or even complete texts, asking yourself, 'What is the main idea of this sentence, paragraph, or text?' Researchers then name phenomena, pose questions, and make comparisons regarding the similarities and differences that can be found within the data.

The raw data come to life as researchers conceptualize about them. As Strauss and Corbin noted, raw data are useless, for you cannot do much with them other than merely count words or repeat what was said. Concepts are always named at previous points of the analysis; they can stem from the literature and do not have to be developed by the researchers. This can be advantageous because some such concepts are associated with analytical meaning, such as 'caregiver burnout', 'experience during illness', and 'loss of status'. However, many of these concepts are already connected to certain theories, which could be disadvantageous to your current study.

---

[4]Barney Glaser and Anselm Strauss founded the tradition of Grounded Theory in 1967 (Glaser & Strauss, 1967), which is not simply a method or an evaluation technique. Strauss later said that Grounded Theory is a research style or a methodology and that at the time, he and his co-author wanted to design an epistemological and political science approach that deliberately and provocatively went against the leading behaviourist research paradigm (see Strauss in an interview with Legewie & Schervier-Legewie, 2004). Kelle sees an 'inductive misunderstanding of one's self' in the beginnings of the history of Grounded Theory (Kelle, 2007b, p. 32). According to Creswell (2010), Grounded Theory developed in three main directions: a) Strauss & Corbin; b) Glaser; and c) Charmaz, who gave Grounded Theory a constructivist flair.

During the first open coding of a text, we recommend that you pay attention to the words and metaphors that the respondents use. In Grounded Theory, such words and statements are referred to as 'in-vivo codes'. For example, Strauss mentioned the term 'tradition bearers of the station', which the head nurse used to refer to another nurse in her unit (Kuckartz, 2010a, p. 75).

In the remaining steps of the analysis process, the Grounded Theory moves from the initial concepts to categories, which are more abstract concepts or summarized concepts on a higher level of abstraction (see Strauss & Corbin, 1996, p. 49). For example, concepts such as 'holding on', 'hiding', and 'moving out of the way' may arise when watching children play. Then, those concepts could develop into the more abstract category 'anti-sharing strategies'.

Concepts within Grounded Theory should be as precise and specific as possible. They are not paraphrases, but they move towards a more abstract, general level. The following examples of concepts stem from Strauss and Corbin (see 1996, pp. 106–107): 'work in the kitchen', 'attention', 'transfer of information', 'unobtrusiveness', 'timing of service', and 'satisfaction of guests'. Once researchers have collected a good number of concepts, they can group them together and summarize them into categories.

Grounded Theory can be seen as an invitation to and instructions for arriving at a theory that is based on the data. The same idea of empirically grounded analysis is true for qualitative text analysis: Every category and subcategory, every relationship presented, every evaluation conducted, and every typology constructed is rooted in the data, documented and traceable for everyone who receives the research, whether they are experts or people who read the research report. From the beginning, Grounded Theory aims to develop *theoretical* categories,[5] however, this is not necessarily the case in qualitative text analysis. Grounded Theory does not require all of the data to be coded because it focuses on moving forward, working with the categories and developing theories, leaving the data behind.

Combining Methods to Construct Categories

Qualitative text analysis is a rule-guided approach and it characteristically combines different methods in order to construct categories in what is referred to as *deductive-inductive category construction*. This can been seen in many of the examples from Mayring and Glaeser-Zikuda's collection *The Practice of Qualitative Content Analysis* (2005), Glaeser and Laudel's approach (2010), as well as the methodically well-documented study 'Family and Right-winged Extremism' by Hopf and colleagues (1995). In the latter, hypotheses and categories are formulated based on attachment theories and these categories are

---

[5]See Kelle (2007c).

then assigned to the data, modified, and differentiated as necessary. At the same time, unexpected elements in the data, such as those that cannot be derived from the attachment theories, serve as inspiration for new categories (see Schmidt, 2010).

Depending on the research question and schedule of a given project, there are different ways to develop categories in a deductive-inductive fashion. The general process is, however, always the same: You start with a category system that only contains relatively few main categories (usually not more than 20) that have been derived from the research question or a theory. Unlike with deductive categories, these categories are seen only as a starting point here. They serve as a search aid, meaning that you can search through the data for relevant content and roughly categorize it. In the second step, sub-categories are then constructed inductively. Here, your search can be confined to the data assigned to each main category.

Chapter 4.3 on thematic text analysis includes a typical example of how categories can be constructed inductively and deductively at the same time.

3.5 The Example Study

In many of the examples throughout the following chapters in which the three basic methods of qualitative text analysis will be described in detail, I will refer to data collected within the framework of our research project, 'Individual Perception of Climate Change – The Discrepancy between Knowledge and Behaviour'.[6] The central research question of this study was: To what extent do people's fundamental assessments, as seen in their world-views, their perceptions of others, and their own positioning in a 'global society', cause the discrepancy between knowledge and behaviour when it comes to protecting the climate? (Kuckartz, 2010b)

The sample consisted of 30 participants that were divided into two age groups: 15–25 years of age ('network kids') and 46–65 years of age ('baby boomers'). The study had two parts: A qualitative, open survey in the form of an interview (1) and a standardized questionnaire (2) that acquired social and statistical characteristics as well as their general assessment of climate change using scales. We started with a problem-centred interview (Mackie, 1974), which was conducted according to the following guide:

---

[6]The study was conducted by students within the seminar 'Environmental Education and Communication' in the winter semester 2008/2009.

>> For interviewers: World-view

In your opinion, what are the largest problems facing the world in the 21st century?

How can we address these problems? Who or what has an impact on them, if at all?

Consider climate change and the necessary CO_2 reductions. Can changing consumption habits in developed countries have a positive effect on such issues?

>> For interviewers: View of others

People often talk about a discrepancy between attitudes and behaviours, such as when a person says one thing, but does another. What do you think causes this sort of behaviour?

>> For interviewers: View of one's self

How do global developments affect you?

How do you think you can impact them? What sort of behaviour impacts them?

Do you actually do that?

Would you like to do more?

Do you feel a sense of responsibility to wrestle with the problems of the 21st century?

>> For interviewers: Closing

Do you think that people can learn how to address these problems? If yes, how? Where?

Figure 3.5   Excerpt from the Interview-Guide of the Example Study

The accompanying four-page standardized questionnaire contained questions regarding the personal relevance of environmental protection, people's assessment of the risks associated with different environmental problems (global warming, nuclear power, etc.), climate change and its causes, as well as regarding personal attitudes towards the environment, communication about the environment, and the individual's level of commitment. In addition, socio-demographic data such as gender, age, level of education, and income were also collected.

The qualitative interviews were transcribed verbatim and the data from the standardized questionnaires were recorded in an Excel table. Both parts of the study were then compiled and analysed using computer-assisted qualitative text analysis. The project serves as a good example for this book because the research question is quite focused and the data from the qualitative interviews is manageable in size. You can imagine how difficult it would be to use the data from a larger project in examples, particularly if they included thousands of pages of interviews that readers would really only be able to comprehend if they had a copy of the data whose scope far exceeds that of this book.

4

Three Basic Methods of Qualitative Text Analysis

In this chapter, you will learn more about:

- The thematic matrix (profile matrix) as a fundamental concept of qualitative text analysis.
- Similarities and differences between the basic types of qualitative text analysis.
- Thematic analysis.
- Evaluative analysis.
- Type-building analysis.
- The basic process and the various phases of these three methods.
- The different methods for preparing and presenting results.

Within social research, there are a number of methods and techniques for qualitative text analysis. Mayring, for instance, distinguishes between eight techniques of qualitative analysis: (1) summary; (2) inductive category building; (3) narrow and (4) broad contextual analysis; (5) formal structured; (6) thematic; (7) type-structured; and (8) scaled-structured (see Mayring, 2010, pp. 113–114).

In the following, three of the basic methods of qualitative text analysis will be described in detail. These three methods use different strategies of analysis and are each used very frequently in research practice. This is especially true for the first type – thematic qualitative text analysis. Interestingly, thematic analysis is also by far the most commonly used method in the field of quantitative content analysis. In this area, it is mostly done as frequency analysis of themes. What distinguishes *qualitative* text analysis from *quantitative* analysis can be seen particularly well in thematic analysis: While the atomizing manner of quantitative analysis aims to convert the verbal data into precise categories (represented by numbers) and then to statistically evaluate the resulting data matrix, qualitative text analysis is interested in the text itself, notably based on the text in its entirety. Even after categories have been assigned, the text itself, i.e. the wording of the statements, is relevant and also plays an important role in the preparation and presentation of results. In quantitative content analysis, however, the results include merely statistical parameters, coefficients, and models, which are interpreted and presented. After the coding process, the verbal data in quantitative content analysis are no longer of interest, even as citations, because the plausibility of the results of the statistical analysis must not be demonstrated using selected text passages.

All three methods of qualitative text analysis described below are both topic-oriented and case-oriented methods. That means they can be viewed not only as category-based analysis but also at the case level as case analysis, e.g. in the form of category-based summaries. The comparison of cases or groups and clusters of cases plays an important role in the analysis process for each of the three methods.

4.1 The Profile Matrix: A Fundamental Concept of Qualitative Text Analysis

The idea of the *profile matrix* is fundamental to qualitative text analysis. In most cases, a profile matrix includes topics (themes) as structuring elements in the columns, so it can also be referred to as a *thematic matrix*. However, it can also include properties, places, dates, etc. Organizing the data in this manner is comparable to creating a cross-tabulation when analysing quantitative data statistically. In quantitative analysis, the parameters and coefficients are of primary interest, the relationships represented in a table are summarized in a single coefficient, for instance Chi-square, Pearson's r or Cramer's V. Of course, qualitative analysis does not aim to identify and summarize numerical values and test for statistical significance; rather, it aims to create a clear and comprehensible interpretation of the information that is included in such a *profile matrix*. The individual cells of the matrix contain not numbers, but text, which you can access at any time during the analysis process. Thus, it is possible to select, separate, and abstract without losing sight of the context.

The profile matrix can be analysed in two directions, as follows.

Horizontally, you can follow a single row of the matrix (for example, the second row, Person 2) to gain an overview of a particular person's statements.

Table 4.1 Prototypical Model of a Profile Matrix, here as a Thematic Matrix

	Topic A	Topic B	Topic C	
Person 1	Person 1's text passages about Topic A	Person 1's text passages about Topic B	Person 1's text passages about Topic C	⇒ Case summary for Person 1
Person 2	Person 2's text passages about Topic A	Person 2's text passages about Topic B	Person 2's text passages about Topic C	⇒ Case summary for Person 2
Person 3	Person 3's text passages about Topic A	Person 3's text passages about Topic B	Person 3's text passages about Topic C	⇒ Case summary for Person 3
	Category-based analysis for			
	⇓	⇓	⇓	
	Topic A	Topic B	Topic C	

This gives you a *case-oriented* perspective structured by the thematic categories of the analysis. The results can take the form of a written case summary for several or all of the selected topics.

Vertically, you can direct your attention to a specific column (for example, Topic B), which gives you a *topic-oriented* perspective. This enables you to view all of the respondents' statements regarding a given topic.

Summarizing one column or one row creates individual case summaries (characterizing one person) or thematic summaries (describing the statements pertaining to the given topic in a systematic manner). However, the matrix can be used for much more complex analyses. You can compare multiple rows with each other, which would compare and contrast different individuals. You can also compare multiple columns with each other, allowing for a comparison of the relationship between different topics, and when their statements correspond with each other. It can also contrast the statements within different categories in order to evaluate how the statements correspond with each other.

Moreover, the rows and columns can be summarized in a vertical as well as horizontal fashion. This means that individuals can be assigned to groups according to specific characteristics, and topics can be grouped under broader or more abstract, over-arching categories.

4.2 Similarities and Differences Between the Three Methods

All three of the methods, described in the following, work with *categories*. Classical content analysis, which was developed as a systematic research method in the 1940s, is essentially based on the idea of creating categories and analysing the empirical material according to these categories. Over time, content analysis evolved more towards a form of quantitative content analysis, which often ignored the qualitative aspect of text analysis, text *comprehension*.[1]

The qualitative methods of text analysis described here in detail are also focused on categories, which are the most important tools of the analysis. The three methods build on each other in some respects, but this should not be interpreted as a hierarchical ranking. Thus, evaluative analysis should not be perceived as superior to thematic analysis and type-building analysis is by no means superior to evaluative analysis. In contrast, it is better to ask which method is more suited to answer a given research question. It is not always beneficial to build types during the analysis. Type-building is often described as a goal of qualitative research in methods textbooks, and it is often viewed as the equivalent to the representative generalizations applied in quantitative research. However, if your goal is to describe the object of your research in detail or to test a hypothesis about how different concepts are related, building types is probably not particularly useful.

Highly explorative or descriptive research will perhaps focus on the analysis of issues and arguments, examining the relationship between categories or, in the style of Grounded Theory, work to create core categories for the phenomena identified in the research field (see Strauss & Corbin, 1996, pp. 100–101). In this case, both evaluative and type-building analysis would not be appropriate. Evaluative analysis would force analysis too early in the process, and both methods follow approaches other than the comparative method of Grounded Theory, which operates mainly in terms of minimum or maximum contrasts.

What do the three methods of qualitative text analysis have in common? Six key points are outlined below:

1   They are methods of analysis, i.e. they do not prescribe a specific type of data collection. Different methods, such as thematic and type-building text analysis, can easily be applied to the same data, for instance, during the secondary analysis of existing qualitative data.[2]
2   They are methods that compress and summarize the data rather than analyse and expand it sequentially in order to interpret it exegetically.
3   They are category-based methods; thus, the analytical categories are the focus of the analysis process, although the way in which the categories are built may vary.

---

[1]This is true for the prototypical computer program 'General Inquirer', which automatically generated a word-based coding of data material. See Zuell and Mohler (1992).

[2]For more information on secondary analysis of qualitative data, see the QUALIDATA Archive in Essex, which can be found online at: www.esds.ac.uk/qualidata/about/introduction.asp.

Categories or topics can be derived from the theory or the research question and carried over to the data, or developed directly grounded on the data. It is quite common to combine various methods to build categories.

4 They are systematic scientific methods and not open to artistic interpretation, meaning the implementation of these methods can be described precisely and mastered by researchers and students. These methods do not involve the art of interpretation that is characteristic in fields such as literary or art history.

5 The three methods are language-related and are initially conceived as methods for systematic qualitative analysis of verbal data. Nevertheless, they may also be applied to images, movies, and other products of culture and communications.

6 Because they are systematic, rule-governed processes, quality standards can be formulated for all three methods. Thus, we can distinguish between a text analysis of better or less quality.

For all three methods, analysis can begin even before all of the data are collected. All three methods are compatible with different sampling methods and can be combined with both more conventional methods, such as a quota-based sampling, and theoretical sampling, as is preferred by Grounded Theory. However, as systematic processes, the three methods require a complete coding of the entire data material, meaning that major changes to the category system require additional processing of the data and are therefore associated with substantial additional effort. The postulate that the entire data of a study can be analysed in a systematic, category-based manner prevents researchers from drawing premature conclusions based on individual cases. Regardless of which analysis method you use, it is recommended that you document the individual steps of the analysis process as accurately as possible in a research journal.

4.3 Thematic Qualitative Text Analysis

Characterization

Thematic qualitative text analysis has been proven and tested in numerous research projects and described in the methods literature in various forms, such as a detailed 'example of a content-reductive analysis' in Lamnek (1993, p. 110). A wide range of methods can be found regarding how to construct the categories with which thematic analysis can be conducted, ranging from creating the categories inductively using the data, to creating the categories deductively based on an underlying theory from the field or the research question.

The extremes of the spectrum of how to construct categories – completely inductively or completely deductively – are rarely found in research practice. In most cases, a multi-stage process of categorizing and coding is used: In the first stage of the analysis, the data is coded rather roughly along major categories, which, for example, have been derived from the general guidelines used in data collection. The number of categories in this first phase is relatively small and manageable; it does not usually include more than about 10 to 20 main categories. In the next phase, the categories are further developed and differentiated based on the data. The entire data set is then coded again, analysed based on the categories, and prepared for the research report. The more elaborate category structure provides a basic structure for the research report. By comparing and contrasting sub-groups of interest, the category-based analysis gains sophistication, complexity, and explanatory power.

In principle, this process allows for the thematic analysis of guideline-oriented, problem-centred, and focused interviews as well as many types of data, such as focus groups or other forms of interviews, including episodic or narrative interviews (see Flick, 2007a, pp. 268–278). Modifications would have to be made for each different type. For example, for a narrative interview, passages of interest might include text passages in which the interviewee tells and explains something; thus, the analysis would largely focus on such narrative data.

Process

The basic process of thematic analysis can be described as follows:

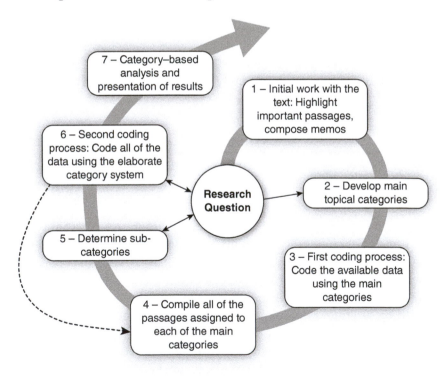

Figure 4.1 Thematic Qualitative Text Analysis Process

Detailed Description

Phase 1: Initial work with the text, highlight important text passages, and write memos

The first steps of the analysis process (initial work with the text, writing memos and initial case summaries) have already been described in Chapter 3; thus, they will only be referred to briefly here. The beginning of the thematic qualitative analysis process is marked by an interested, careful reading of the text and selection of particularly important text passages to highlight. You can record comments and observations in the margins and create memos to record things that strike you as particularly interesting or relevant as well as any ideas you may have regarding the analysis. At the end of this first phase of working through the text, you can write an initial, short case summary.

In the next step, the thematic categories are determined, meaning that the first coding process can begin.

Phase 2: Develop main thematic categories

The actual content of the text, i.e. the topics and sub-topics included, serve as analysis categories in thematic qualitative text analysis. Where do these topics come from? How do you choose the 'right' topics and sub-topics for the analysis? How many topics should be included for analytical differentiation?

The main topics can usually be derived directly from the research question and have often already impacted the way in which data was collected. Since respondents in our example study were asked in an open interview what they view as the largest problems in the world, it is only logical that 'largest problems in the world' serves as a main category for our analysis. The same is true for the topic 'individual behaviour towards climate change': Because this point is central to the entire research project, it is included in the research question and serves as one of the main topics for the analysis. It is possible that researchers may discover new, unexpected topics through their careful reading of the text. It is best to approach working with the text as you would approach open coding in the Grounded Theory: by writing notes regarding the new topics in the margins and/or memos. As a rule, you should record anything that seems relevant or peculiar at first; as you work through the data, you will gain a better sense of how to distinguish between random topics and topics that could be significant for the given analysis.

Whether you develop the topics and sub-topics directly using the data and according to the procedures described in Chapter 3, or rather deductively based on the theoretical framework of the research question or the general guidelines of the given study, you should first process some of the data in order to check if your topics and sub-topics and other definitions can actually be applied to the empirical data. Just how much of the data material should be included in such a test depends on the size of the entire data set and the complexity of the category system. The more complex the data and the greater the number of categories, the more data material should be included in the trial run. In general, 10–20% of the data should suffice to initially test the applicability of the topics and categories. If you develop the categories empirically and based directly on the data, you can skip this initial test and proceed directly with the actual coding process.

Phase 3: First coding process – Coding all of the data using the main categories

The *first coding process* is conveniently designed in a sequential manner, meaning that researchers work through the text section-by-section and line-by-line from beginning to end, to assign text passages to categories. Thus, researchers must determine which topics are being addressed in a given passage of text and assign it to the appropriate category. Passages that do not contain information pertaining to the pre-determined topics and sub-topics are irrelevant for the research question and should remain uncoded.

As a rule, categories should be assigned according to the overall assessment of the text, especially when researchers are uncertain. Hermeneutically speaking, in order to understand a text as a whole, you have to understand its individual parts. Because one text passage can include multiple topics, it is possible to assign it to multiple categories.

> In thematic qualitative text analysis, one text passage can refer to different main and sub-topics. Thus, one passage can be assigned to multiple categories. As a result, some of the coded passages will overlap and intertwine with each other.

Classical content analysis' demand for precisely defined categories is often misunderstood to imply that a text passage can only be assigned to one category. This is only true for category systems that are designed in such a way that sub-categories exclude each other (see the example of deductive category building in Chapter 3.4). In thematic coding, it is assumed that a given text passage can refer to multiple topics and thus be assigned to multiple categories.

In our example project, we developed categories using the general thematic structure of the interviews:

Abbreviation	Main Thematic Category
WP	Largest problems in the world
IP	Impact on world problems
CC	Consumption and global climate change
CD	Causes for discrepancy between attitudes and actions/behaviour
PR	Personal relation to global developments
PB	Personal behaviour
SR	Sense of responsibility
AL	Ability to learn regarding how to approach global problems

Figure 4.2 List of Main Thematic Categories

The following rules apply to the category system used in the first coding process of a thematic analysis. The category system should:

- be established in close connection to the research question and goals of the given project;
- not be too detailed or too broad;
- contain a precise, detailed description of the categories;
- be formulated with the report of results in mind. For example, categories should be selected that are suited to give structure to the research report at the end of the analysis process; and
- be tested on a section of the data material.

The entire data set is coded during the first coding process. You must determine the size of the individual coding units, i.e. the text segments to be coded. The following excerpt from an interview addresses this issue.

I: In your opinion, what are the largest problems in the world in the 21st century?

R1: Well, that's a totally broad question (...) I would definitely say that religious and cultural conflicts are some of the most difficult, and of course the environment and natural conflicts, because, well, I believe you can't really rate them because all the conflicts are affecting the world and they are very deeply rooted (...) From conflicts about water to religious conflicts, there are many, many conflicts! But I think the environment and cultural and religious conflicts are currently the most serious.

The passage clearly falls under the category of 'WP – The largest problems in the world'. The coding unit should be large enough that it can still be understood when it is taken out of its original context. If the answers to a guideline-oriented interview are relatively short, they can be coded quickly if the entire answer to a given question is coded as a unit. The whole section pertaining to a given topic, which could contain multiple paragraphs, should then be assigned the code 'WP – The largest problems in the world'. This approach prevents the same category from being assigned to the same section or paragraph of text repeatedly. It is possible that other topics and categories could be mentioned in the middle of this section, in which case those individual sentences would be assigned a second category.

The following rules for coding, i.e. how to assign text passages to categories, can be formulated:

1 Units for coding are not defined by formal criteria, but by semantic boundaries. Thus, these units of meaning should always be complete thoughts and full sentences.
2 If a unit of meaning contains multiple sentences or even paragraphs, these are to be coded together.
3 If interview questions or clarifications are essential for understanding the respondent's statement, they should be included in the coding.
4 When assigning categories, it is important to develop a good sense of how much text surrounding the relevant information should be coded. The most important criterion for this is that the given passage must still be understood when taken out of its context.

Working in a team: Ensuring the quality of the coding process

In the practice of qualitative text analysis, an important question is whether a text should be coded by one single coder or by multiple (at least two) coders. Hopf and Schmidt (1993) recommend a co-operative approach called consensual coding. This is a technique in which two or more members of a research team code interviews independently. This requires a category system where the categories and sub-categories are well described and explained with examples. Consensual coding improves the quality of the research project and the reliability of the coding.

In the first step, two or more coders code the data independently. Then, in the second step, the coders sit together, sort through the codes, and check for similarities and differences. After discussing their reasoning, they should aim to find a consensus regarding the most appropriate coding. By doing so, researchers can often fine tune their category definitions and codings, using the disputed text passages as prime examples.

If they are unable to reach a consensus – which is very rare – they should call in more members of the research team or discuss the disputed passages with the entire team. This process makes differences in coding and evaluation visible and can lead to constructive discussions within the research team. Unlike any issues with coding agreement that may arise in the course of a quantitative text analysis, where the main concern is to get a satisfactory coefficient of intercoder reliability, the focus here is on clarifying the discrepancies as a group and coming to a consensus. Consensual coding requires at least two different researchers who are involved in the coding from the very beginning.

Thus, it is generally advisable to work with two or more coders who code the material independently from each other. The category definitions will almost automatically become more precise and the text assignments to them more reliable, if the data are coded by multiple researchers. However, it will not always be possible to work with multiple coders, for example, if you are writing a Master's thesis or dissertation you often don't have others to support you. If this is the case, researchers should carefully look to improve explicit category definitions and prototypical examples where necessary. There is little doubt that coding by only one person is unfavourable and should be avoided. It may be an exception if the coding-scheme contains only a few well-described main categories as is the case with a transcript of a guide-structured interview. Here the coder would not have to make any real decisions regarding the correct assignment of categories since the answers always belong to the corresponding question of the interview-guide which is taken as the coding scheme in the first coding process.

Phase 4: Compile all of the text passages that belong to the same main category and Phase 5: Create sub-categories inductively based on the data

As a rule, following the first coding process, the next step in a thematic analysis should be to create sub-categories for the relatively general main categories. This process generally includes:

- Selecting the thematic category that you would like to differentiate, i.e. the category for which you would like to create (new) sub-categories.
- Compiling all of the coded text segments that belong to this category into a list or table. This is called *text retrieval*.

- Creating sub-categories based on the data. Add the sub-categories to a list, which is initially not yet ordered. When working in a team, each researcher can be responsible for suggesting sub-categories for parts of the data. If you are in a team of four and have conducted, for instance, 20 interviews, then each researcher should work trough five cases and make suggestions.
- Systemizing and ordering the list of sub-categories, identifying the relevant dimensions, and, if necessary, summarizing the sub-categories into more general and more abstract sub-categories.
- Formulating definitions for the sub-categories and illustrating these using prototypical examples.

First example: Creating sub-categories for the category 'WP – Largest problems in the world'

In our example project, we created sub-categories for the category 'WP – Largest problems in the world' based on the data material. We initially collected everyone's proposals for the sub-categories during a team meeting. Next, we systematized and grouped all of the global problems that were named.

How does one convert such a large list into a solution that is suitable for the further analysis? In general, you must take the goal of the analysis into account. You have to ask yourself: What would I like to report on this subject later in my research report? How detailed can I and should I be at this point? Do I need the sub-categories to establish relationships between the categories? What degree of differentiation is useful and necessary?

In this example, we as a research team assumed that what the respondents mentioned as the world's most important current problems are closely related to personal attitudes and, therefore, influence people's actions in everyday life. With respect to the main topic of the study, namely the individual's perception of climate change, we also wanted to investigate whether mentioning global climate change as one of the largest problems in the world has an impact on the individual's everyday actions. Categories should be clear and concise: as simple as possible, as sophisticated as needed; the greater the number of sub-categories, the more precise the definition must be; the greater the susceptibility to incorrect coding, the more complex the coder training and the more difficult it is to achieve intercoder agreements. Generally, for the sake of completeness, all categories should also include an extra sub-category entitled 'Other'.

In the example project, our final list of sub-categories appeared as follows:

Table 4.2 Definition of the Sub-Categories within the Main Category 'Largest Problems in the World'

Sub-Categories of "Largest Problems in the World"	Definition	Examples from the Data
Environment	Includes changes and conditions that affect the environment in terms of natural environment.	Climate change Environmental pollution
Conflicts	Includes all non-violent and violent conflicts between states and different social, political, ethnic, or religious groups.	War Terrorism Religious conflicts
Problems in Society	Includes social changes and problems at different levels of society.	Social change Egotism Moral deterioration of society Migration
Disease	Includes extensive problems that are caused by illness.	Epidemics
Technology	Includes technical changes today that affect our lives forever.	Changes in technology
Scarcity of Resources	Includes any shortage of goods that are necessary for survival or for maintaining certain social standards.	Starvation Water shortages Raw material shortages Energy shortages
Poverty	Identifies poverty conditions in a global context as well as within the context of their own culture.	Child poverty
Social Injustice	Does not focus on aspects of poverty, but rather emphasizes the unjust distribution of wealth or the gap between rich and poor. Can also relate to equal opportunities, such as educational opportunities.	Gap between rich and poor Inequality: 1st, 2nd, 3rd world
Other Problems		

Second example: Behaviour towards climate

The second example of how to identify dimensions and create thematic sub-categories is slightly more difficult. This time, we are going to process the main category 'personal behaviour regarding climate change'. Begin by closely reading the text passages that were coded during the initial coding process. Then, code the concepts and themes openly until you figure out how to systematize and identify dimensions. In this case, we noted a long list of codes including:

- Drive a fuel-efficient car
- Separate trash/recycle
- Buy energy-saving light bulbs
- Solar panels on roof
- Industry should be a role model
- We could certainly do more
- No time
- No money to buy organic
- Individuals cannot really do anything
- Buy energy-efficient appliances
- Only technology can really make a difference
- Political-correctness
- Save energy
- Not the environmentally-conscious type
- Too comfortable/easy to fall into old routines
- Developing morals is more important than the environment.

Systematizing and summarizing such a seemingly endless list of useful sub-categories requires some skill and practice, but most importantly, it should pertain to the research question, bear the final product of the study in mind, which, in most cases, is the research report, and be suited to the given recipient or audience. The classification system should be plausible, easy to communicate, include current theoretical considerations, and push for broader theoretical differentiations. If you choose to rely on existing concepts and categories, you should attempt to further differentiate and systematize them to fit your study.

We identified four dimensions within the main category 'Personal behaviour to protect the climate':

1 *Current behaviour.* The areas in which respondents indicated actively aiming to protect the environment were defined as sub-categories. These included: 'save energy', 'separate trash/recycle', 'buy energy-efficient appliances', 'use environmentally-friendly modes of transportation', 'commitment to environmental conservation groups', 'drive fuel-efficient cars', and a residual category 'other'.
2 *Willingness to change behaviour.* In principle, nearly all of the respondents were willing to do more to protect the climate; however, most formulated their own readiness by saying 'Yes, but...' and listing excuses for not following through. Their arguments and obstacles were defined as sub-categories, including: 'not enough time', 'too comfortable (in my old ways)', 'one person is not enough', 'industry and government should be role models', 'everyday routines get in the way', 'too expensive', 'public infrastructure is insufficient', and a residual category 'other'.
3 *Philosophy of behaviour.* This dimension refers to the general attitude conveyed by many respondents regarding personal behaviour and/or changing personal

behaviour. Personal action occurs amidst the tension between two central points: On the one hand, 'ecological correctness' exerts pressure to act and is perceived as such by almost all respondents. On the other hand, people experience a desire to maintain their own habits, particularly in self-defined core areas. This tension led many respondents to make statements regarding their own personal behaviour based on their principles. As a result, we defined sub-categories that represent mottos and mentalities, such as 'Managers and political leaders should be role models', 'Start slowly by taking little steps', 'If others do not change, I will not either', 'Technology does not bring substantial change', 'I do not think about stuff like that', and 'We must all behave properly'.

4   *Associated areas of behaviour.* The fourth dimension was defined by the areas of behaviour that the respondents named. This dimension partially overlaps with the first dimension 'current behaviour'. The purpose for defining an independent dimension was to establish which areas of behaviour were mentioned within the context of climate behaviour, regardless of whether one is currently doing something or would be willing to act (change his or her behaviour) in this area in the future. The manner in which such sub-categories were formed here is similar to the course of action outlined for the 'largest problems in the world'. The sub-categories are consistent with the sub-categories of the current behaviour dimension; a precise definition should be formulated for each sub-category.

Phase 6: Second coding process – Code all of the data using the elaborate category system

After successfully defining sub-categories and dimensions, you can proceed to the second coding process, in which you assign the coded text passages within each main category to the newly defined sub-categories. This is a systematic step of the analysis that requires you to go through the data again. It is important to ensure that a sufficient amount of data is used to differentiate the main topics and define new sub-categories. If researchers create the categories on the basis of a small selection of the data, they often find it necessary to extend and re-define the sub-categories later in the analysis process. While it is easy to summarize and to merge sub-categories later in the process, defining new sub-categories later proves to be more problematic since it would require you to go through and re-code all of the data again later. This, of course, is detrimental since it would require significantly more time and effort.

If the data is quite voluminous or you have already started the analysis process and established sub-categories, you can shorten the first few phases of the analysis process by assigning text passages directly to the appropriate sub-categories, thus eliminating the initial coding process using the main categories. Be pragmatic and take the sample size into consideration when determining how many dimensions or sub-categories are suitable for your project. For example, it would make little sense to establish a large number of sub-categories or characteristics for a project containing relatively few respondents. This is especially true if you plan to create and analyse types following the thematic analysis, as the focus of type-building is on the similarities and differences between respondents. The defined characteristics should be found in several of the sample cases, not unique to individual cases.

The **seventh phase** of the analysis process is important and quite substantial; thus, it will be described separately later in this section. Beforehand, however, it seems beneficial to review systematic summaries of each case.

Case-Related Thematic Summaries

After completing the second coding process, you have essentially structured and systematized the data and you can begin the next phase of the qualitative text analysis. It can be useful to add an intermediate step in which to create thematic summaries of the data which have been structured in the previous phases of the qualitative text analysis. This approach is especially helpful when you are dealing with an extensive amount of data or when the text passages assigned to any given topic (such as 'personal behaviour') are scattered throughout the entire interview.

Creating case-related thematic summaries, especially for the purpose of comparative tabular summaries, is an approach that is common in qualitative analysis and well-represented in methods literature (e.g. in Miles & Huberman, 1995). Ritchie and Spencer (1994) as well as Ritchie, Spencer and O'Connor (2003) present a detailed form of this approach within the realm of applied political research, which they refer to as 'framework analysis'.

The thematic matrix serves as a starting point and is virtually transformed by the systematic process into a thematic matrix whose cells no longer contain passages from the original material, but analytical summaries written by researchers. Through this step of systematic thematic summary, the material is compressed and reduced to what is really relevant for the research question. The following process results:

Step 1 – Starting point: The thematic matrix

Systematic coding produces a thematic grid or matrix. Each cell of this matrix represents a node that is assigned to a position or passage in the data, which can be scattered throughout the entire interview. The previous phases of the

Table 4.3 Thematic Matrix as Starting Point for Thematic Summaries

	Topic WP – Largest problems in the world	Topic PB – Personal behaviour	Topic C	
Person 1	Person 1's text passages about Topic World's Problems	Person 1's text passages about Topic Personal Behaviour	Person 1's text passages about Topic C	⇒ Case summary for Person 1
Person 2	Person 2's text passages about Topic World's Problems	Person 2's text passages about Topic Personal Behaviour	Person 2's text passages about Topic C	⇒ Case summary for Person 2
Person 3	Person 3's text passages about Topic World's Problems	Person 2's text passages about Topic Personal Behaviour	Person 3's text passages about Topic C	⇒ Case summary for Person 3
	Category-based analysis for			
	⇓	⇓	⇓	
	Topic WP	Topic PB	Topic C	

content analysis process produce an unorganized form, or permutation, of the interviews within the categorical framework of the researchers. The more complex and elaborate the category system is, the more difficult it is to present it in a (printable) thematic matrix.

Step 2 – Creating case-related thematic summaries

In this step, researchers create summaries for the topics and sub-topics. The summaries should be paraphrases of the text in the researchers' words, not direct quotes from the text. This requires more effort on the part of the research team; however, it aids in the analysis process since it forces you to reduce one person's actual statements to their core and summarize them in light of the research question.

Let's look at an example in the above thematic matrix: column 'PB – Personal behaviour' for Person R2. The cells of this matrix are filled with the coded statements from seven passages within the interviews of the example project. The coded passages are presented in Figure 4.3, in which the numbers of the first and last paragraphs pertaining to each statement are listed in the first two columns.

These statements were summarized as follows:

from	to	
P	**P**	**Text Passage**
26	26	Yes, as I said, I would just live more energy-efficiently; I think that's the only way. Or just that the big energy companies rely more on nuclear power, of course, but the general public doesn't really approve of that. (...) Otherwise, yes, just as I said regarding driving – to use more public transportation or ride a bike for short distances (...) Yes.
27	28	I: Do you actually do that or not really? R2: No, I personally do not. I have to say that I'm pretty easy-going and live quite comfortably and like I said, I am not really sure that we are responsible for the drastic changes in the climate in the first place.
32	32	OK, first you'd have to make it really clear to me that we really are the culprit. Maybe there has always been climate change in nature. I mean, Germany used to have a thick layer of ice on the ground and, yes, the ice has indeed melted, so the climate has again changed and that's just how things go, the climate is constantly changing. For me, it would have to be really clear that we are the main reason that the climate is currently so altered.
33	34	I: Yes, and what do you think now, for example, of conscientious consumption? Meaning, for example, buying organic food or Fair Trade clothing. Do you think that's a good thing in principle? Would you buy organic, perhaps, if you knew more about it? Or do you think organic is the same as normal fruit and vegetables, so you don't really see the point? R2: Well, organic, I would buy some organic products really just for my health because I don't know how much that really influences the environment. Um, Fair Trade clothing, I don't know, I just buy the clothes I like. So I wouldn't necessarily buy something just because it is fair trade. If it looks good, I might prefer to buy it, perhaps to give poorer people a chance.
36	36	Yes, in principle, I know that. Things are, I don't know, produced in the low-wage countries where people make a measly salary and sold in Europe or in general in the West, for a higher price. (...) Um, I don't know if (...) that I if I choose to stop [buying such things] it will change much.
38	38	Yes, I just think (...) that I am the type of person who (...), what would the people down there do if they had no job at all. That's what I think. And if I don't buy the clothes, then maybe they would not be able to work at all and then they would still be worse off, even if they work for next to nothing down there.
49	52	I: So if you were to see, for example, that the people around you are doing their part, for example, your friends or the people that you interact with the most, would you change your opinion and participate and work to combat climate change or would you still be virtually 'the black sheep'? R2: I think that I would still be the black sheep. (laughs) I: Aha. So you feel rather strongly about it? I mean, you don't think that anyone could influence you to change your mind? R2: Yeah, I don't know. I think it would be a little like (...) I mean, sure, there's a known group dynamic, but (...) I don't think I would do something like that just because other people are if I weren't completely convinced. That proves that it isn't really better.

Figure 4.3 Coded Text Passages as Starting Point for Thematic Summaries

Person R2 makes no effort to consider the connection between his personal behaviour and protecting the climate. The reasons he gives for this are that it is questionable whether climate change is driven by human activities and it is also questionable whether one can really change anything by, for example, buying Fair Trade products. Moreover, his own convenience and comfort are the deciding factors. Even if many of the people around R2 are environmentally-conscious, he would see no reason to change his behaviour. Potential areas for behavioural change are identified in the subjunctive: save electricity, use public transportation, ride a bike, and buy organic products (but only for health reasons).

It is not necessary to create case-related thematic summaries for every single topic and sub-topic. You may certainly focus on the topics that you find especially relevant and for which you would like to create comparative case overviews later in the analysis process.

Step 3 – Case overviews

Ultimately, developing thematic summaries assists researchers in presenting case overviews (in the form of tables) later, in which you can compare several interviews with each other in regard to selected categories. Such an overview contains the case summaries in the cells of the thematic matrix, as can be seen in Table 4.3.

It should be noted that creating theme or topic-oriented summaries represents a very effective step of the analysis because it requires comprised, analytical paraphrases of the original data. The summaries also enable researchers to present and compare the results in a different manner ('data display'). Case summaries and comparisons (see next section) are made possible by this step of the analysis, especially considering the fact that it would be impossible to create such overviews using original quotations and passages from the text due to space reasons. Moreover, the comprised and abstract overviews have more analytical power and evidence. Thus, the described approach has many advantages:

- It is systematic, not episodic since all cases and coding units are handled in the same manner.
- The summaries are based on original statements; thus, they are literally *grounded in empirical data*.
- The analysis covers all areas, for all of the data that pertains to a given topic is included in the analysis.
- The analysis is flexible and dynamic; researchers can add, expand, or edit at any point during the analysis process.

- The analysis is well documented and it is easy for other researchers to understand which original statements led to which summaries.
- The thematically-oriented summaries are a very good preparation for subsequent forms of analysis, such as the detailed individual interpretation ('within-case analysis') or the cross-case analysis ('between-case analysis') (see next section).
- If the analysis is carried out using QDA software, connections are established within the thematic structure between summaries and original data, which allows quick access to both.

Category-based Analysis and Presentation of Results

The second coding process, or the intermediate step of creating case and topic-related summaries, is followed by the **seventh phase** of the analysis process: Analysis and Presentation of Results. In thematic qualitative text analysis, the focus is, understandably, on the topics and sub-topics. There are seven different types of analysis, which are arranged clockwise in the following figure:

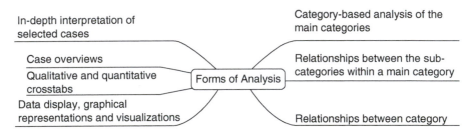

Figure 4.4   Seven Types of Analysis and Presentation of Results in Thematic Qualitative Analysis

1) Category-based analysis of the main categories

The initial results for each main thematic category (the columns of the profile matrix) should be reported in the first part of the research report. It may be helpful to ask, 'What do respondents have to say about this topic?' and 'What do they leave out or only mention briefly?' During this descriptive step of the analysis process, the categories should be ordered in a reasonable manner that the reader can follow, not simply in the order that they are presented in the category system or in alphabetical order.

If thematic sub-categories were formed, such as for the major categories 'Largest problems in the world' and 'Personal behaviour to protect the climate' in the above example, the sub-categories should also be presented. Important or interesting numbers from the research should be included. For example, it may be important for readers to know whether '3 of 39' or '29 of 39' respondents consider 'environmental and climate problems' some of the largest problems in the world today. Instead of merely presenting the frequencies with which topics and sub-topics are mentioned in the interviews, the report should present content in a qualitative manner, which can also include assumptions and interpretations on the part of the research team. For example, while it is important to know that nine respondents consider 'economic and financial problems' some of the largest problems facing the world today, it is even more important to know which economic problems were named and the words respondents used to describe them. It can be seen in our study, for example, that economic and financial problems are only referred to very generally; respondents mention the 'financial crisis' or the 'economic system'. Prototypical examples should be cited in the research report, which can be written once all of the segments for a given sub-category have been read and structured according to content.

2) Relationships between sub-categories within a main category

The relationships between thematic categories and sub-categories can be analysed and described in two different ways: within the main categories and/or between them. When analysing within the main categories, you can examine the relationships between the sub-categories. This involves naming the sub-categories by determining which problems in the world are named most frequently and which ones are seldom or never mentioned. How do the respondents formulate their answers? Do they mention other sub-categories within their answers? For example, do they mention poverty or other specific topics in statements about 'social inequality'? Can you identify patterns or clusters in their answers?

3) Relationships between categories

Analysing the relationships between main categories allows for a larger-scale analysis. You can compare two categories, such as the most frequently named problems in the world and the respondents' sense of responsibility, or extend your analysis to include a comprehensive analysis of the complex relationships between multiple categories.

4) Qualitative and quantitative crosstabs

Crosstabs can be used to examine correlations between characteristics, such as socio-demographics, and coded thematic statements. For example, you could use a table to compare how men and women indicate a sense of responsibility or to compare the respondents' level of education or income. Crosstabs present the verbal, qualitative data in a systematic manner. Because crosstabs can also contain numbers and percentages, they can also indicate how often specific groups of respondents named specific categories or sub-categories. For example, using a crosstab, you can figure out how often specific groups of respondents named the sub-category 'largest problems in the world'.

5) Graphical representations and visualizations

Diagrams can be used to gain overviews of sub-categories. For example, you could present all of the behaviours that the respondents name as environmentally-friendly behaviours in a diagram. If you are interested in the specific numbers and distributions of such behaviours, you can create a bar graph or a pie chart. Mind-maps can be used to present respondents' reasons for not changing their behaviour. Graphs can even be used to compare selected individuals or groups with each other.

6) Case overviews

It can often be very useful to create case overviews, which compare a selection of cases with each other with respect to characteristics that are deemed especially relevant to the research question. Huberman and Miles (1995, pp. 172–206), Schmidt (2010, pp. 481–482), Hopf and Schmidt (1993, p. 16), and Kuckartz et al. (2008, pp. 52–53) present instructive explanations of how to create case overviews. A case overview is very similar to a thematic matrix; however, it only includes selected topics or categories.

Case overviews provide a perfect basis for an analysis. Thus, Hopf et al. (1995, p. 30) and Schmidt (2010) recommend:

> ...preparing case summaries, which represent an important initial step in the analysis of individual cases because they facilitate the comparative analysis based on selected cases. They aid in selecting which individual cases to further analyse (according to the principles of theoretical sampling). They also aid in the controlled, disciplined, comprehensive interpretation of results by preventing distortive or theoretically coherent but presumptive summaries. Case overviews enable researchers to test their hypotheses on the bases of multiple individual cases. (Hopf & Schmidt, 1993, p. 15)

The rows of a case overview can be arranged to suit the given analysis. For example, you can arrange it so that individuals with similar characteristics appear next to each other in the table. It may also be useful to indicate numbers and frequencies, for they reveal even more information about the data, including whether a phenomenon or collection of phenomena occur frequently or should be considered as unique cases. It must be noted that the numbers here are fundamentally different than the numbers you would use within the framework of statistical tests in studies with representative samples where the goal is to identify standard, universal statements. However, scientific knowledge about relationships does not require representative samples. If it did, a good deal of medical and pharmaceutical research would be meaningless.

7) In-depth interpretation of selected cases

Case overviews arranged like spreadsheets are a good starting point or backdrop for individual case studies because they give you a sense of how each person compares to the others and where they each fall on the spectrum. Particularly interesting individuals can be included in the research report in the form of in-depth interpretations (see Schmidt, 2010). To create an in-depth interpretation of an individual case, you have to re-read the transcript carefully, concentrating on a specific topic or question:

> At the end, responses are formulated that refer to this individual case. Depending on the question at hand, these responses can consist of detailed or concise descriptions, contextual evidence of relationships, or theoretical conclusions. In-depth interpretations can be used to verify existing hypotheses or assumptions, to come to new theoretical conclusions, or to question, extend, or modify the theoretical framework. The technique used depends on the interpretation of the question and the respective tradition to which the researchers feel connected, e.g. the hermeneutic or the psychoanalytic. (Schmidt, 2010, pp. 482–483)

The rules for in-depth interpretation of individual cases are not as strict as those for tabular summaries and interpretations presented in the previous steps. Here, researchers are free to choose between different models of interpretation like hermeneutic or psychoanalytic-oriented techniques (as noted above).

Drawing conclusions

Every report of results should come back to the original research question. Did the study answer the research question sufficiently? Have any assumptions or hypotheses been confirmed or rejected? Which questions could not be answered using the data at hand? Are there any gaps in the research or in the study as a whole? Which questions arise regarding your own research? What new questions or issues emerged during the research process?

Documenting the analysis

The entire analysis process should be documented in the report. To do so, researchers must illustrate the steps of the analysis process, explain how categories were constructed and describe the extent to which the categories and sub-categories were based on the data. The category system should not be withheld from the readers. If it is too large to include directly in the report, it should be included in the appendix at the end of the report. Coding rules and prototypical examples should also be documented in the appendix, or even on a CD-ROM that accompanies the report. Examples of coding rules and prototypical examples for some of the categories can be included in the methods section to illustrate the methodological approach.

4.4 Evaluative Qualitative Text Analysis

Characterization

Evaluative qualitative text analysis is another basic method of systematic qualitative data analysis. It is used in many projects in empirical research and well-represented in methods literature. In his book *Qualitative Content Analysis*, Mayring presented a detailed description of this method (see Mayring, 2010, pp. 101–109). Unlike in thematic analysis, which focuses on identifying, systematizing, and analysing topics and sub-topics and how they are related, evaluative qualitative analysis involves *assessing, classifying, and evaluating content*. Researchers or coders assess the data and build categories, whose characteristics are usually noted as ordinal numbers or levels. Mayring presents a detailed example of this method in his example from the project 'Unemployment of Teachers'. In this example, each respondent is assessed using the evaluative category 'self-confidence', which contains the characteristics 'high self-confidence', 'average self-confidence', and 'little self-confidence' (see Mayring, 2010, pp. 105–107).

In some cases, nominal or interval scales can also be used in conjunction with evaluative text analysis, as evaluative analysis does not strictly require characteristics to be defined by ordinal scales or levels. After the evaluative coding process, you can use the categories to explore assumptions regarding correlations as well as test any initial hypotheses on the data, such as by the use of crosstabs. In evaluative analysis, the coders' language and interpretation skills are important – even more so than in thematic qualitative analysis. To a certain extent, Osgood's 1940s content analysis model[3] served as a precursor to evaluative qualitative text analysis; however, in practice, Osgood's very formal and detailed approach, which he described as *Evaluative Assertion Analysis*, is very different from the type of evaluative qualitative analysis practised by researchers today.

Mayring's approach of a scaling and structured analysis also demonstrates a more quantitative orientation, for it strictly transforms text into numbers and ultimately leads to a statistical analysis. In contrast, Hopf and Schmidt focus

---

[3]For more about Osgood's model, see Krippendorff (2004, pp. 177–178) and Merten (1995, pp. 193–199).

on a detailed interpretation of the text rather than on a statistical analysis (Schmidt, 2010).

Process

Formally speaking, evaluative qualitative text analysis contains the same main phases as thematic qualitative analysis, including:

- Working with the text
- Building categories
- Coding
- Analysing
- Presenting results.

In thematic analysis, categories are created using topics and sub-topics, which impact the following phases of the analysis. Evaluative qualitative analysis is different, as can be seen in the following diagram, which presents the typical evaluative analysis process on the basis of one single evaluative category. When analysing multiple categories, simply proceed through Phases 2 through 5 for each category:

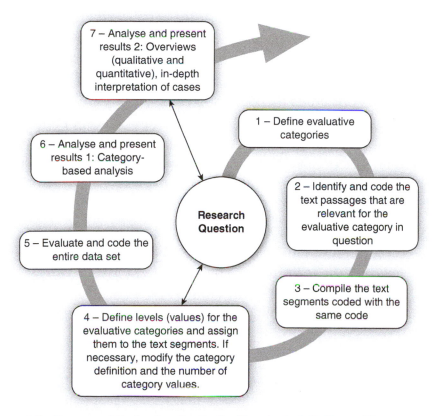

Figure 4.5 Process of Evaluative Qualitative Text Analysis in Seven Phases

Detailed Description

The individual phases of the evaluative text analysis process can be described as follows:

Phase 1: Define evaluative categories

The first phase of the analysis involves determining the category or categories for the evaluative analysis. Where do the categories come from? Why do you wish to evaluate or assess these categories rather than simply including them as thematic categories? General information regarding building categories was presented in Chapter 3. Whatever the case may be, there must be a strong connection between the categories or types of categories and the research question. For example, one particular category may have already played an important role when you formulated the research question and collected the data. Take, for instance, the category 'sense of responsibility' in our example project. As you can imagine, researchers examining individual and societal perceptions of global climate change often encounter people's 'responsibilities' or 'sense of responsibility'. It would be quite difficult to discuss such a topic without addressing personal or societal responsibility. Thus, it would be foolish to act like you discovered the category for the first time when you analysed the data. Such a category is supported by the data, but it was not discovered or developed within this research project. Of course, researchers may discover other suitable categories during the analysis process, which would then represent new discoveries.

In order to decide whether the category 'sense of responsibility' should be used as an *evaluative* category, you could consider the fact that it is believed that expressing one's sense of responsibility is an important influencing factor and that it may be worthwhile to compare it to other thematic categories over the course of the project, such as 'individual behaviour towards protecting the climate'.

Because it requires a good deal of time and effort to create and code an evaluative category, you should carefully consider your reasons for conducting an evaluative coding of a given category. Moreover, you must ensure the data enables you to conduct this assessment for all respondents (possibly with a few exceptions). Select only those categories for evaluative coding that are particularly important to the research question.

Phase 2: Identify and code those text passages that are relevant to the evaluative category in question

The entire data set is processed in this phase. Every text passage that contains information pertaining to the given category – such as to the interviewee's sense of responsibility – must be coded. Concerning the question of how to determine the size of a text segment to code, the same considerations apply as in thematic qualitative analysis (see Section 4.3). If a category has already been coded thematically, you can build on previous codings and save time by skipping the second phase of the evaluative coding process. One evaluative category could conceivably integrate multiple thematic categories.

Phase 3: Compile text passages coded with the same code

Like in thematic analysis, this step includes a category-based analysis. All of the text passages that belong to a given category are compiled by case. This means that all of the thematically relevant passages (from one respondent) are compiled into a list or table, which serves as the starting point for the analytical work in the following two main phases of the analysis.

Phase 4: Define values (levels) for the evaluative categories and assign them to text segments. If necessary, modify the category definition and the number of category values

In order to determine a category's characteristics, you have to read a sufficient number of text passages and decide how detailed you would like to make the category distinctions. At the very least, you should differentiate between three characteristics, including:

- highly characteristic of the category (high level)
- relatively uncharacteristic of the category (low level)
- unable to classify, meaning that a given respondent cannot be classified according to his or her characteristics using the information provided.

The third characteristic ('unable to classify') is almost always necessary in evaluative qualitative text analysis since the data often does not contain sufficient information about every thematic aspect for every respondent in the sample.

During this phase of the analysis, you also have to determine whether you would like to evaluate the respondent's text as a whole or the individual text passages separately. In the end, the goal of evaluative qualitative text analysis is usually to evaluate the respondent's entire text. If the number of passages is manageable, we recommend evaluating the entire text at once.

Phases 4 and 5 comprise a process that may have to be repeated and refined through several cycles, for the characteristics should be defined and then applied to a section of the data to test their practicability and applicability. If necessary, changes can be made to the definitions and differentiations between characteristics. It can be difficult to define hard and fast rules regarding how much data is required to determine and test characteristics. If you are dealing with a large number of cases (respondents) (n > 100), a selection of 10% and 20% of the cases should be sufficient. However, you should be careful not to select respondents or groups of respondents systematically, i.e. do not select only women or interviewees belonging to a specific socio-demographic group.

If the sample is composed of distinct groups (such as the age groups 15–25 and 45–55), you should include a representative selection from each group, such as five from the younger group and five from the older group. In most other cases, a random selection would be better.

Constructing an evaluative category in the example project

One of the main research questions in our project 'Perception of climate change' addressed the extent to which an individual's sense of responsibility influences his or her actions or behaviour in protecting the environment as well as his or her assessment of other people's actions. Thus, the category 'Sense of responsibility' was selected for evaluative analysis. It should be noted that in our study, one's sense of responsibility refers to one's willingness to take responsibility at some point in the near future, not one's accountability in a legal sense.

Several variations of how to define characteristics were developed and tested in our project. Two of the variations, which include three and five characteristics, respectively, are presented in Tables 4.4 and 4.5:[4]

Table 4.4 Definition of the Category 'Sense of Responsibility' with Three Characteristics

Characteristic	Definition	Notes for Coders
A1: Sense of responsibility exists	Subjective conviction to take responsibility for the problems connected with global climate change.	The majority of the statements indicate a sense of responsibility, which is articulated in the first person (I, me).
A2: No sense of responsibility	No subjective conviction to take responsibility for the problems connected with global climate change.	The statements indicate little or no sense of responsibility. Impersonal language (people, you) and subjunctive are used.
A3: Unable to classify sense of responsibility	The topic 'responsibility' is mentioned, but the individual's personal attitudes towards it are unclear or not articulated.	The individual's sense of responsibility cannot be determined using the text passages.

---

[4]Both tables only contain a few selected citations as examples.

The first way of defining evaluative categories consists of, in essence, the dichotomous characteristics 'Sense of responsibility exists' and 'No sense of responsibility'. The third characteristic is allotted for ambiguous or unclassifiable cases or respondents. The advantage of using this minimalistic variation with only three characteristics is that there is only one differentiation that has to be made, which can be articulated by precise definitions and fitting prototypical examples. The disadvantage associated with this type of definition is that the less differentiated assessment of the data will lead to limitations in subsequent phases of the analysis. In contrast, selecting five different characteristics produces a more detailed assessment (see Table 4.5).

Table 4.5 Definition of the Category 'Sense of Responsibility' with Five Characteristics

Characteristic	Definition	Prototypical Example	Notes for Coders
A1: High sense of responsibility	Subjective conviction to take responsibility for the problems connected with global climate change.	No prototypical example	All of the statements indicate a sense of responsibility, which is articulated in the first person (I, me).
A2: Moderate sense of responsibility	Some or varied subjective conviction to take responsibility for the problems connected with global climate change.	No prototypical example	Many, but not all of the statements indicate a sense of responsibility.
A3: Low sense of responsibility	Little subjective conviction to take responsibility for the problems connected with global climate change.	'I only feel somewhat responsible because I don't have kids and I don't plan to (...) I am sure I would think differently if I had kids, but otherwise, I think it doesn't really matter to nature whether there are people or not...'	The majority of statements indicate little sense of responsibility. Impersonal language (people, you) and subjunctive are used.
A4: No sense of responsibility	Subjective conviction <u>not</u> to take responsibility for the problems connected with global climate change.	'No, I personally do not.'	All of the passages indicate very little or no sense of responsibility.
A5: Unable to classify sense of responsibility	While the topic is addressed, the individual's personal attitudes remain unclear.	'...If I think about it yeah, but if I just live my life, I know that the responsibility is there, but I don't really feel it directly...'	Ambiguous or contradictory statements.

While testing the applicability of these characteristics on our data, it became evident that 'high sense of responsibility' was never assigned because the coding rules were so strict. The same is true for the fourth characteristic, 'no sense of responsibility', which was never assigned since it could only be coded if a person specifically indicated feeling 'no sense of responsibility'.

Given the relatively small number of interviews to analyse (n = 30), we pragmatically decided to only distinguish between three characteristics plus the characteristic 'unable to classify sense of responsibility' if there is insufficient information. The characteristics were then defined as follows and provided with prototypical examples.[5]

Table 4.6 Final Definition of the Category 'Sense of Responsibility' with Four Characteristics

Characteristic	Definition	Prototypical Example	Notes for Coders
A1: High sense of responsibility	Subjective conviction to take responsibility for the problems connected with global climate change. - Person clearly states: 'I feel responsible' and reflects on his or her own involvement. - Reference to behaviour: Conviction to contribute something to improve the problems connected with global climate change (and not expressed in subjunctive). - Names specific actions and behaviours, which do not only refer to small-scale efforts such as picking up litter or cigarette butts off the street.	'Definitely. The problems of the 21st century, that's a huge concept, a huge thing and I clearly feel a responsibility. First, I feel responsible for my immediate environment because that's where I can act. If I feel responsible for some huge flooding disasters that are increasing in the world in the 21st century, I wouldn't really know where to start or what to do. But when I see that our soil is eroding, then I definitely feel a responsibility to do something to prevent it. If I buy something, then I buy it from people who are working to preserve the land from which we gain our food.'	All three aspects within the definition must rate predominately high. It must be recognizable that the person is referring to him or herself (Indicator: using 'I' and 'me' instead of 'people' or passive constructions.)

[5]This and the previous table only contain a few selected citations as examples. For space reasons, we have omitted source information for the prototypical examples.

Characteristic	Definition	Prototypical Example	Notes for Coders
A2: Moderate sense of responsibility	Some or varied subjective conviction to take responsibility for the problems connected with global climate change.	'Yes, like I said, if I think about it yeah, but if I just live my life, I know that the responsibility is there, but I don't really feel it directly that it is connected to certain behaviours...'	Include context if the reference to behaviour is unclear.
	Recognizes the need for acting responsibly in principle; however, sometimes he or she feels responsible and acts accordingly and sometimes he or she does not. Responsibility is often transferred to others (e.g. politicians).	'I think we as citizens can't do as much as perhaps more responsible people, such as politicians or the government or perhaps the European Union, which would probably know better and could do more to address the problems anyway.'	
A3: Low sense of responsibility	Little or no subjective conviction to take responsibility for the problems connected with global climate change. Only somewhat aware of the problem. The language is rather defensive. Little awareness of actions. Often expresses conviction that he or she cannot do much to help solve the problems.	'I only feel somewhat responsible because I don't have kids and I don't plan to (...) I am sure I would think differently if I had kids, but otherwise, I think it doesn't really matter to nature whether there are people or not...' 'No, I don't feel responsible. I am just not receptive to that. It's all about (...) I mean, I don't feel an inner desire to get more involved, especially in terms of environmental matters.' 'No, I personally do not. I have to say that I live comfortably and I don't really know if we are the ones who are responsible for the drastic climate changes.'	Pay attention to use of subjunctive and avoidance of first person ('I' and 'me').
A4: Unable to classify sense of responsibility	The individual's personal attitudes remain unclear or are so contradictory that they are impossible to characterize as high, moderate, or low.	---	Include context where necessary.

Phase 5: Evaluate and code the entire data set

This phase includes the final category-based assessment and evaluative coding of the entire data set. In our example project, this means that we assessed each person's personal sense of responsibility and assigned it one of the given characteristics, which we then recorded in the data set.

If you are uncertain how to characterize a given case, make note of why the person could be characterized one way and not another. It is easy to do this using memos, which you can assign to specific text passages. As before, this phase of the analysis does not merely involve mechanical coding; rather, coders should stay alert and look for especially relevant passages or examples to include in the research report. It is not uncommon to discover that the definitions of characteristics must be more precise or illustrated using additional examples. Any uncertain cases should be discussed with the entire research team.

Phases 6 and 7 of evaluative text analysis are described in the next section.

Types of Analysis and Presentation of Results

Similar to preparing and presenting the results in thematic qualitative analysis, it is advantageous in evaluative qualitative text analysis to proceed from more basic to more complex types of analysis. We can distinguish between seven different types of analysis, which are presented clockwise in the following figure.

The diagram shows the different options of analysis (clockwise). The first two types are mainly descriptive and focus on single categories. They are done in Phase 6 of the analytic process.

Phase 6: Analyse and present results 1: Category-based analysis

Descriptive Analysis: Verbal presentation of the evaluative categories and their characteristics

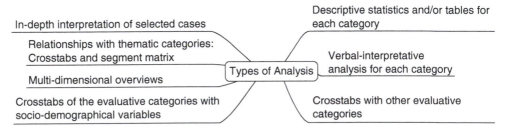

Figure 4.6 Seven Types of Analysis and Presentation of Results in Evaluative Qualitative Text Analysis

The research report typically begins with a simple, descriptive presentation of the evaluative categories. The analysis process should be documented at the beginning of the presentation of results. This includes presenting the categories created and the theories they reference and documenting the process used to build the categories.

In the following excerpt of a report, the categories, selected characteristics, and their content are described. In the above example, this would mean that the first three levels of sense of responsibility are presented with examples (see table above).

Descriptive analysis within a single category

Each evaluative category's results can be presented in two manners:

a) *Statistical tables*

- How frequently the characteristics of an evaluative category appear; in absolute frequencies and percentages, i.e. how many people demonstrate a high, moderate, or low sense of responsibility.
- Presentation of the frequencies of characteristics as a graph, such as in the form of pie charts or bar graphs.
- Overview tables with the respondents listed in the columns, in which a characteristic is noted for each person.

b) *Verbal-interpretive*

- Presentation of what was said, in what way, and using which arguments (e.g. regarding the topic of responsibility); sorted by characteristic.
- Presentation of general and extraordinary statements, the latter of which are usually found in marginal characteristics. For example, the person who is completely ignorant regarding climate change is in the group 'People with little or no sense of responsibility'.

Phase 7: Analyse and present results 2: Qualitative and quantitative overviews, and in-depth interpretations of cases

A variety of analyses follow the descriptive presentation of individual evaluative categories, including bivariate and multivariate correlation analyses, summary tables, and in-depth interpretations of cases.

a) Crosstabs with other evaluative categories

Traditional crosstabs, such as those used by statistical analysis programs, can be used to investigate the correlations with other evaluative categories. The result is an arrangement of two evaluative categories in the following manner.

Table 4.7   Crosstab of Two Evaluative Categories

Personal behaviour to protect environment	Sense of Responsibility			
	High	**Moderate**	**Low**	**Total**
Yes	Number of people with positive personal behaviours and a high sense of responsibility	Number of people with positive personal behaviours and a moderate sense of responsibility	Number of people with positive personal behaviours and a low sense of responsibility	Total number of people with positive personal behaviours
No	Number of people with negative personal behaviours and a high sense of responsibility	Number of people with negative personal behaviours and a moderate sense of responsibility	Number of people with negative personal behaviours and a low sense of responsibility	Total number of people with negative personal behaviours
Total	Number of people with a high sense of responsibility	Number of people with a moderate sense of responsibility	Number of people with a low sense of responsibility	

The cells of the table can contain the absolute frequencies, meaning the number of respondents, as well as percentages. Such a table contains valuable, descriptive information, even if there are only a limited number of cases. If there are a large number of cases and each cell contains a sufficient number of cases, you can also calculate statistical coefficients (Chi-squared calculations) and measures of association.

b) Crosstabs of the evaluative categories with socio-demographic characteristics

The associations between evaluative categories and socio-demographic variables can be presented in crosstabs in a similar fashion; the socio-demographic variable simply takes the place of the second evaluative category. Crosstabs could be used to answer questions like, 'Are there gender differences evident in people's sense of responsibility?' or 'Do an individual's level of education, social status, or other social characteristics influence their sense of responsibility?'

Table 4.8 Crosstab – Evaluative Category and Socio-Demographic Variable

Sense of Responsibility	Gender		Total
	Male	Female	
High	Number of males with a high sense of responsibility	Number of females with a high sense of responsibility	Total number of people with a high sense of responsibility
Moderate	Number of males with a moderate sense of responsibility	Number of females with a moderate sense of responsibility	Total number of people with a moderate sense of responsibility
Low	Number of males with a low sense of responsibility	Number of females with a low sense of responsibility	Total number of people with a low sense of responsibility
Total	Total number of males	Total number of females	

These questions can be answered using statistical tables and methods in which the correlations are presented in crosstabs. In Table 4.8, the relationship between sense of responsibility and gender is presented. Again, if there are enough cases included, you may compute statistical coefficients and parameters.

c) Overview tables: Multidimensional relations of multiple categories and socio-demographic characteristics

Overview tables, which organize the respondents' answers by categories or socio-demographic variables, can be used to identify constellations of characteristics at one glance. Such tables serve as the basis for identifying patterns and enable researchers to gain an overview of selected questions within the greater research project. The case overview presented below, in which the respondents comprise the rows, shows whether or not a given respondent considers natural and environmental problems to be some of the largest problems in the world today (thematic sub-category), to which age group the person belongs (socio-demographic variable), how the person was classified in terms of his or her sense of responsibility (evaluative category), and gives a characteristic statement regarding his or her personal behaviour (thematic category) in the form of a quote directly taken from his or her interview.

Table 4.9 Overview Table

Case	Largest WP: Natural and Environmental Problems	Age Group	Sense of Responsibility	Statements regarding Personal Behaviour
Person 1	No	15–25	low	'basically, I know that. (...) I don't think much will change if I stop...'
Person 2	Yes	46–65	low	'I think I should be fine for the rest of my time on this planet. (...) Otherwise, I think it doesn't really matter to nature whether there are people or not...'
Person 3	Yes	15–25	high	Intentionally environmentally-conscious. However, 'sometimes my hands are tied for financial reasons'.
Person 4	No	15–25	low	Throws little trash away (i.e. recycles); drives a fuel efficient car.

d) Relationships with other thematic categories: Crosstabs and segment matrix

Matrices can also be used to present the relationships between evaluative and thematic categories. Crosstabs, like the two presented above, can be used to present numerical relations, which only take into consideration whether or not the given thematic category or sub-category was coded. For example, the table indicates whether respondents currently consider 'natural and environmental problems' to be some of the largest problems in the world. Then, you can reconstruct this kind of dichotomous crosstab to include two columns, as in the above example 'Sense of Responsibility by Gender'.

You can also create another, more detailed matrix called a segment matrix, which is presented in Table 4.10. The goal here is not to aggregate all possible interactions in numerical form, rather to examine the original text passages that have been coded with the thematic category.

This matrix can be used to record assumptions and guide future research. For example, you could ask: Is there a link between taking responsibility and a respondent's future plans (such as a lake house)? Do all of the egotistical

Table 4.10   Segment Matrix

	Sense of Responsibility		
	High	**Moderate**	**Low**
Food/Diet	Text passages pertaining to the eating habits of people with a high sense of responsibility	Text passages pertaining to the eating habits of people with a moderate sense of responsibility	Text passages pertaining to the eating habits of people with a low sense of responsibility
Transportation	Text passages pertaining to the modes of transportation that people with a high sense of responsibility use	Text passages pertaining to the modes of transportation that people with a moderate sense of responsibility use	Text passages pertaining to the modes of transportation that people with a low sense of responsibility use

people without children who do not plan to have a family have a low sense of responsibility?

e) In-depth interpretations of selected cases

Like in thematic analysis, in-depth interpretations of selected cases represent a reasonable ending point of the analysis work within evaluative analysis (see Section 4.2). After summarizing and consolidating the data in the previous phases of the analysis, you can now turn your attention back to the individual cases. On the one hand, you can interpret their statements and meanings and explore their particularities; on the other hand, the individual case will also be examined as an exemplary 'case of...' for analysing regularities (see Schmidt, 2008).

Evaluative or Thematic Analysis?

In comparison, evaluative text analysis appears more hermeneutic-interpretive than thematic analysis. Assessments are conducted on the case-level; thus, this kind of analysis is more holistic because it generally analyses the case as a whole rather than assessing individual passages. However, you can also code using more detail by evaluating and coding each of the individual coded passages before integrating them into the overall analysis, which gives them an overall score. It is questionable if this is more effective in practice, for researchers often like to (or must) include broader context in order to evaluate text passages correctly. From a hermeneutical standpoint, it would be difficult to justify not taking the entire text into consideration and simply focusing on the statements directly surrounding the given text passage. However, by including the broader context, you can assess the entire text in relation to the given category.

The classifications and assessments to be made in evaluative qualitative text analysis demand more of the coders than in thematic analysis. It is hard to imagine that coders could come to agreement without having specialized knowledge in the field of research. Coders must understand what they are doing and be able to justify their codings using the data. We recommend working with at least two independent coders in evaluative analysis. Of course, there may be situations in which analysts must work alone, such as when writing a thesis or dissertation; however, it is beneficial to contemplate when a second person may be pulled in to assist you or double-check your work.

In general, the categories (and sub-categories) tend to be broader in evaluative analysis than in thematic analysis. The evaluative approach is especially suitable for theory-oriented research. This does not necessarily mean that you have to have profound theoretical knowledge regarding the research question and seek to investigate explicit hypotheses, as you may very well gain more insight regarding hypotheses and theories after beginning the research process. In any case, evaluative qualitative analysis is especially suitable for theory-oriented research; it is less appropriate for descriptive research.

Of course, it is also possible to combine evaluative qualitative text analysis with thematic analysis and define evaluative categories only for particularly interesting themes or topics. In some cases, the evaluative categories could build on the thematic coding and make use of the work already done on the text. Evaluative qualitative text analysis is a method that clearly demonstrates that qualitative research is not only suitable for explanatory research. Often you can hear the opinion that qualitative research is good for generating but not for testing theories. This statement describes the mainstream of qualitative research, but it's not a statement that is always true without exception. Hopf et al. (1995) argue that standardized questionnaires with predetermined answers are often inadequate in social research because they cannot express the complexity of the research question. So, also in theory-testing research, it may be useful to let respondents answer in their own words with whatever nuances they may demonstrate and then analyse their responses as a research team and try to reconstruct the level of the evaluative category or categories. This approach often promises more valid information and data than standardized tests and instruments.

Also in evaluative qualitative analysis, the analysts can follow the case-oriented perspective in the form of in-depth interpretations of individual cases.

In addition, crosstabs may present an overview of the data – of thematic as well as evaluative categories; however, they cannot be compared with those based on a large number of representative studies.

The following section presents type-building qualitative text analysis as a way to move from thematic and/or evaluative analysis to the construction of typologies.

4.5 Type-Building Text Analysis

According to many qualitative methodologists, creating types and developing a typology are the main goal of qualitative data analysis (see Creswell & Plano Clark, 2011, pp. 212–214; Kluge, 2000; Lamnek, 2005, pp. 230–241; Schmidt, 2000)[6]. You can build types in a methodically controlled manner using qualitative text analysis. Such a type-building analysis is more complex and methodically demanding than thematic or evaluative analysis. For this reason, the following chapter begins with a characterization of the approach's methodological foundations.

The real core of type-building involves searching for multi-dimensional patterns and models that enable researchers to understand a complex subject or field. The type-building analysis often builds on the preliminary work done in thematic or evaluative coding.

Tradition of Type-Building in Social Research

Methods for building types are used in many qualitative studies[7] and there are numerous suggestions in social research methods literature for how to analyse qualitative data using systematic, empirical approaches to building types.

Constructing typologies and thinking in terms of types were already important to the classical social psychology research of the 1930s. Widely known is the field research project about an Austrian municipality, *Marienthal: The Sociography of an*

---

[6]There are more entries for the term 'type' and its derivatives ('type-building', 'typology', 'typification', etc.) than almost any other word in the index of Lamnek's textbook, *Qualitative Social Research*. For more on typologies, also see Kelle & Kluge (2010) and Kluge (1999).

[7]Approaches for building types can often be found in biography research, in youth research, in lifestyle research, and in interdisciplinary research fields such as public health and environmental awareness and attitudes.

Unemployed Community.[8] This study used a variety of methods to collect data – including observation, interviews, time sheets, and more (see Jahoda, Lazarsfeld, & Zeisel, 2002) – and to create detailed descriptions of each of the 100 families who participated in the study. Many factors were taken into consideration, which emerge as a guideline for describing the families of the sample:

- Family (composition of the family, age, income, property)
- Home visit protocol (description of the apartment and furnishings and their respective condition, impression of children)
- Husband's life story (biography, education, occupation/career, position, political orientation, hobbies)
- Wife's life story (biography, education, occupation)
- Interviews (attitudes, basic orientations, political views, future perspectives)
- Observations (behaviour of individual family members, daily life/structure, visit to restaurant, activities)

By constantly comparing and contrasting the individual cases according to the above criteria, researchers were able to identify four different mindsets for dealing with unemployment and responding to the deprivation it caused (Jahoda et al., 2002, pp. 64–82):

- The *unbroken* continue their daily life and household, search for a new job, and stay active and happy.
- The *resigned* maintain their daily life and household, but do as little as possible and refrain from making future plans.
- People *in despair* have lost hope and are moving backwards; they make little effort to improve their situation and do not even bother to look for work.
- The *apathetic* have lost the energy to take care of their home and their children; they are like passive bystanders to what is happening to them and do not even try to change their situation.

These mindsets were precisely based on the data and their characteristic features were named explicitly, as can be seen in the following excerpt from the description of the 'resigned':

> If we list the buzzwords that lead us to classify a family as 'resigned', we would include: no plans, no future perspective, no hope, major limitations in taking care of anything beyond daily life, including maintaining the household, taking care of the children, and maintaining a sense of relative well-being. (Jahoda, Lazarsfeld, & Zeisel, 1975, p. 70)

---

[8]This study was conducted towards the beginning of the 1930s by the Research Unit for Economic Psychology at the University of Vienna under the direction of Paul Lazarsfeld and Marie Jahoda. See http://agso.uni-graz.at/marienthal/e/pictures/15_ marienthal_study.htm.

Looking back at the history and development of empirical social research, we not only find practical applications for building types, but also works that reflect on the methodical foundations of type-building, such as Bailey (1973, 1994), Hempel and Oppenheim (1936), Kelle & Kluge (2010), Kluge (2000), Kuckartz (1991), Lazarsfeld (1972), Schutz (1972) and Weber (1978)[9]. Schutz examined everyday life and concluded that 'an individual's everyday knowledge about the world is a system of typical aspects' (Schuetz, 1972, p. 8). According to Schutz, all of the knowledge that comes with experience is organized in the form of typical experiences. We do not experience our surroundings and environment 'as an array of discrete, one-time objects that are distributed over space and time, but rather as "mountains", "trees", "animals", "humanity"' (ibid, p. 8f). Types are often constructed in anthropology, though the basic aim there is to understand types in a psychological sense of understanding individuals' inner lives. In social science research, the goal of analysis is simply to understand what is typical. Schutz follows the tradition of Max Weber, who declared that constructing comprehensive types was the main goal of empirical social science research. Types as analytic devices link hermeneutic methodology, which aims at understanding individual cases, with social science statistics, which aims to find standard interrelationships and correlations.

Characterization of the Type-Building Approach

A general definition of type-building is: Elements are grouped by type (cluster) according to how similar they are in terms of selected attributes and characteristics. The elements of each type – i.e. usually persons in social research – should be as similar as possible and the different types should be as un-alike and heterogeneous as possible.

Thus, within empirical research, type-building refers to grouping cases into patterns or groups that differ from the other groups or patterns surrounding them. A type always contains several (individual) cases that are similar to each other. All of the types that are used to describe a given phenomenon are called a 'typology'. Therefore, according to its definition, a typology always contains several types and their relationship to each other; it structures the types according to similarities and differences.

Types are the result of comparing and contrasting cases; thus, they are different from inductive conclusions based on individual cases. Characteristically, type-building aims to differentiate rather than develop a general theory. It is based on cases, not variables or characteristics, meaning that cases are examined and grouped according to their similarities. The objects to be analysed and grouped do not have to be people; for example, you could also analyse

---

[9]Unfortunately, most of the literature is not available in English.

institutions or organizations, or even group arguments according to typical patterns of thought.

The Concept of Attribute Space

Defining an 'attribute space' is fundamental to type-building. Typologies are based on several (at least two) characteristics or attributes, which constitute an n-dimensional attribute space (see Barton, 1955).

For illustration purposes, we can take a look at the simplest form: a two-dimensional attribute space. For example, let us consider a diagram that presents 'environmental awareness' by 'environmental behaviour' in which a given number of respondents are presented as data points of the measured values on the two scales. The types within this kind of typology contain elements with identical attributes and characteristics, meaning individuals with the same characteristics. A simple example of such a typology presents a four-field table based on two dichotomous attributes. The table below stems from Peter Preisendoerfer's research (1999, p. 98):

Table 4.11 Preisendoerfer's Simple Typology of Environmental Awareness and Behaviour

		Environmental Behaviour	
		Positive	*Negative*
Environmental Awareness	*High*	Type 1: Consequent protector	Type 2: Environmental rhetorician
	Low	Type 3: Uncommitted protector	Type 4: Ignorant to environment

This type of diagram allows us to build types quite easily. The types correspond to the cells of the table – in this case, there are four. The task of the researchers is now to formulate meaningful labels, e.g. 'consequent protector' or 'environmental rhetorician'.

The social milieus in lifestyle research, such as the prototypical milieus used by SINUS Institute,[10] are good examples of a complex, four-dimensional attribute space. There, one of ten social milieus can be selected for a given household. Regardless of the method used, each type is – implicitly or explicitly – based on the notion of an attribute space.

---

[10]See www.sinus-institut.de/en (accessed 27 November 2012).

Forms of Type-Building

In both qualitative and quantitative research, the process for building empirical types contains five phases:

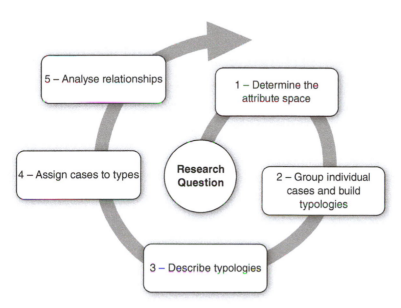

Figure 4.7   Five Phases of Empirical Type-Building

Phase 1: Determine attribute space

In this first stage of the analysis, researchers must define the attribute space that serves as the basis for type-building.

Phase 2: Group individual cases and build typologies

In the second phase, typologies are constructed, i.e. cases are grouped into clusters (types). After comparing and contrasting the typologies, you can decide which typology is best suited to the data. This phase is thus an experimental phase. Several solutions for grouping the individual cases are tested and compared.

Phase 3: Describe typologies

The constructed typologies and the individual types that have been created are described in greater detail in this phase.

Phase 4: Explicitly assign individual cases to the created types

The fourth phase focus shifts from the groupings back to the individual elements. Here, individual cases (usually respondents) are assigned finally to the created types.

Phase 5: Analyse relationships

In the final phase, typologies and the different types within them are presented according to their characteristics and the relationships between the types and secondary variables are analysed.

The first phase of building types involves deciding which attributes are relevant for the desired typology and determining what information is available in the data that has been collected. In the above example of mindsets from the Marienthal study, all of the attributes that were used to describe the families were relevant to the typologies. The number of attributes you can include in your type-building depends on the construction of the typology. There are three main approaches for constructing typologies:

a) Building types with homogenous attributes ('monothetic types')

This option for type-building is shown in Table 4.11. Assigning a particular participant to a particular type, such as Type 2 'Environmental rhetorician', for example, is only suitable if both attributes are indicated in the appropriate levels. Thus, since Type 2 is defined by a high level of 'environmental awareness' and negative 'environmental behaviour', all of the respondents assigned to this type must indicate high awareness and negative behaviour towards the environment. All four types of the typology show no variance; internally, they are perfectly homogenous. The disadvantage of this kind of homogenous attribute typology is that it simply allows researchers to work with relatively few attributes and characteristics. Even using three attributes with four characteristics each would produce 4 x 4 x 4 = 64 homogenous attribute types.

b) Building types by reducing the diversity

Homogenous attribute types can be pragmatically reduced to a manageable number using a method described by Lazarsfeld. The table below illustrates just how to do so. There, all possible combinations of parental level of education are presented in a 4 x 4 table with 16 cells.

The 16 different combinations are not only difficult to grasp, but also difficult to work with in an empirical study, for example, if presenting how educational background impacts the environmental awareness of teenagers.

It makes more sense to reduce the diversity of the 16 cells to a more manageable number of types. To do so, you must order the combination of attributes and reduce the number of combinations so that the typology of parental educational level, for example, only contains five types, which are illustrated in Figure 4.8 below:

	Father's Level of Education			
Mother's Level of Education	No degree	Middle School	High School	College
No degree	Type 5	Type 4	Type 3	Type 2
Middle School	Type 4	Type 4	Type 3	Type 2
High School	Type 3	Type 3	Type 3	Type 2
College	Type 2	Type 2	Type 2	Type 1

Figure 4.8 Building Types by Reducing the Diversity

The five types can be summarized as follows:

- Type 1: Both parents graduated from college.
- Type 2: One parent graduated from college.
- Type 3: One parent graduated from high school
- Type 4: One parent graduated from middle school
- Type 5: Neither parent finished school.

Two of the created types, specifically Type 1 and Type 5, are homogenous in terms of attributes, meaning that both parents of all of the respondents within the type have the same level of education. In the case of Type 1, both parents graduated from college; in the case of Type 5, neither parent finished school. The other types created via reduction (Types 2, 3, and 4) show variance, for they contain respondents with different attributes, in this case different levels of parental education. For example, five different attributes can be assigned to Type 3. The determining factor is that one parent graduated from high school; the other parent could have graduated from high school, middle school, or never have finished school.

c) Building types with heterogeneous attributes ('polythetic types')

The first two forms of type-building are referred to as 'artificial types' because they are constructed without direct reference to the empirical data; they are *constructed* by combining attributes and characteristics. Some combinations may not even exist in reality (such as 'Mother graduated from college' and 'Father did not finish school'). 'Natural types', on the other hand, are built directly using the empirical data, meaning that respondents are grouped according to types, which are as homogenous as possible internally and as heterogeneous as possible externally. Such types are almost always polythetic; the individuals that belong to a type are not absolutely the same in terms of the attributes within the attribute space, but they are quite similar.

Natural typologies can be ordered according to systematic, intellectual structures as well as using statistical algorithms. Cluster analysis methods are especially suitable for the latter (see Kuckartz, 2010a, pp. 227–246). A good way to build complex polythetic types without such formal algorithms is to systematically process and group case summaries, as presented in the five phases in Figure 4.9.

Phase	Task
1	Define attribute space and create a case summary for each respondent that is focused on these attributes.
2	Sort, order, and group case summaries according to similarity.
3	Decide on a reasonable number of types to be built.
4	Formulate creative names for each type that poignantly express the main characteristics of each type.
5	Assign each respondent to a type; order the respondents according to their similarity to the central type.

Figure 4.9 Type-Building: From Case Summaries to Typologies

In research practice, you can implement this method by writing each case summary on a note card and asking the research team to arrange these cards (which represent respondents) on a large bulletin board. To do so, proceed as follows:

Preparing for team meeting

1   Distribute the case summaries evenly among members of the research team.
2   Each researcher must now review the cases that have been assigned to him or her closely, checking the case summary and revising it as necessary before writing it on the note card.

Working as a group

1   As a group, determine the nature and scope of your typology.
2   Each researcher should then present his or her cases to the group and pin them to the bulletin board according to how well they correspond or relate to the cases that have already been pinned on the board.
3   Eventually, arranging and re-arranging the cards in this manner will make clusters evident.
4   Once all of the cards have been placed on the board, discuss any remaining uncertainties within the group. Then, assign each cluster a fitting title and colour.

Constructing, arranging, and assigning an order to types in this way represents a creative act and will not produce a precise, canonized description. Here are a few helpful tips: It is often useful to work through this type of categorizing and typifying task as a group. Case summaries can be noted as bullet points on note cards and then pinned to the board as the group aims to find meaningful labels for types.

Process

The type-building qualitative text analysis process differs in many respects from thematic and evaluative analysis. The type-building process begins with

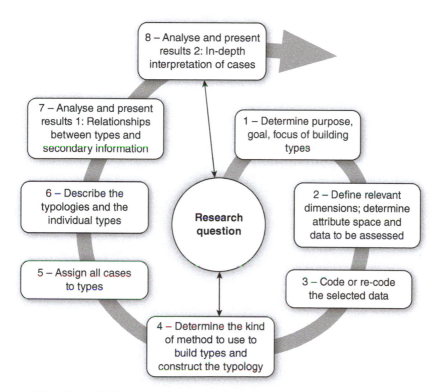

Figure 4.10   Type-Building Qualitative Analysis Process

considerations regarding the goal and purpose of building types. Several differ-ent typologies could be constructed within one project. For example, one typology could demonstrate how information is handled regarding the risks of atomic energy and another could demonstrate how atomic energy risks were communicated regarding the Fukushima disaster. As a rule, the attribute space is constructed using categories and variables that have already been estab-lished; if new categories are created as types, they will have to be coded first. If this is the case, the thematic and/or evaluative analysis methods described above can be implemented.

Figure 4.10 shows the detailed process of type-building content analysis, which basically follows the process of social scientific type-building men-tioned above.

Detailed Description

Phase 1: Determine purpose, goal, focus of building types

The first step to building types is to determine what exactly you would like to accomplish by building types. You must also determine how complex the typol-ogy should be and how many differentiations are necessary within it. In addition, you should consider how important primary and secondary attributes and char-acteristics are to your own research interests as well as the research question. Attributes that are essential for building types and form the basis of the attribute space are considered primary attributes; secondary attributes are other charac-teristics that are influenced by or related to the typology. If, for instance, you would like to create a typology for environmental awareness and examine the impact of an individual's personal behaviour towards the environment, behav-ioural dimensions should not be included in the typology because that would result in a tautological analysis of the impact of behaviours on behaviours.

Typologies can be constructed to be quite complex or quite simple, i.e. you can select a large or small number of attributes for the attribute space, which determines the complexity of the typology. For example, the typology 'Mentality towards the climate' would demand a complex attribute space of which the typology 'Personal behaviour to protect the climate' would only comprise one part. Other typologies, such as knowledge, attitudes, and per-sonal behaviour, would also be included.

Phase 2: Define relevant dimensions, determine attribute space and data to be assessed

The next step to building types involves deciding which of the attributes that are empirically based on the data are seen as relevant for the typology. Selecting the relevant attributes should be based on the project's theoretical framework and/or focused on the research question. In the Marienthal study, attributes were selected according to their potential relevance for a typology of mindsets. After a few visits in the field (i.e. the village of Marienthal), the researchers developed a feeling for factors that influence how people cope with unemployment. These attributes, which were essential to the mindsets (types), were selected. These included: manage household, take care of children, search for a new job, active lifestyle, future perspectives, etc.

To determine the attribute space, you can rely on the existing thematic and/or evaluative codings or use the previous information available about the respondents (such as socio-demographical or biographical data). It is recommended to limit the selected attributes to those that pertain to a sufficient number of respondents. The attributes and characteristics will be used to differentiate the types; thus, it makes little sense to select attributes that only apply to two of 40 respondents since that means that 38 of 40 respondents are identical. The concept of attribute space requires a manageable number of attributes, assuming you would like to create a pure typology or a typology based on a reduced number of attributes. A larger number of attributes is only suitable if you would like to create a polythetic typology by grouping the case summaries together or using an automatic method of classification (such as cluster analysis).

Qualitative interviews are characterized by the fact that not all interviews include information regarding potentially relevant attributes, especially if the interviews are conducted without a structured guideline. In such situations, it is advisable to select a less complex attribute space that contains fewer attributes because researchers may have difficulty grouping the available information reliably into types. If, for instance, the data only contains information about household management for a few of the respondents, it makes little sense to select such an attribute as a primary attribute for constructing the typology, even if it is theoretically considered significant. In some situations, such as field studies, it may be possible to ask further questions and gather the missing information.

The second phase of building types is closely associated with the first. Here, you must re-examine the data at hand to concretely determine if and in what form the desired information is available.

Thus, you must determine if you can rely on existing thematic and/or evaluative categories or need to create new categories based on sections of the material, which will be coded in the next phase.

Phase 3: Code or re-code the selected data

In most cases, type-building analysis builds on a previously conducted thematic or evaluative coding. If this is the case, type-building analysis is quite easy to perform since you can build on the existing thematic and/or evaluative categories. If you have not conducted a previous analysis of the data, you must begin by coding the data to your selected attributes and characteristics according to the processes and rules described in thematic and evaluative coding.

In some cases, it might be necessary to add an intermediate step to this phase of the analysis. For example, assuming that the texts have been coded thematically and all of the passages that refer to household management have been assigned to an appropriate category, you may now wish to further classify the attribute 'household management' according to a three-level scale: (1) Manages household as usual; (2) Partially manages household; and (3) Neglects household. First, we now need to review each case and assign the correct values before we can continue constructing the typology.

If you have collected socio-demographical attributes for the respondents (such as information about their biography, age, educational level, career, etc.), perhaps using a survey, you can use these attributes and characteristics to create the types.

Phase 4: Determine the kind of method to use to build types and construct the typology

Before you begin the actual process of grouping and creating types, you should think about the number of types that would be suitable for your research question and data. First, consider whether any natural groups exist in the field. Then, consider the number of respondents included in the study. If you are dealing with a relatively large number of respondents, such as in the case of the Marienthal study, which included over 100 families, you can use a greater degree of differentiation (i.e. more types) than in a smaller sample of, say, 20 respondents. Other important factors to consider are the practical relevance of your study and how well you can communicate your typology within the scientific community. When building types and selecting a suitable number of types, you should always keep your audience in mind: readers, reviewers, and recipients. Of course, it is not imperative to determine the suitable number of types *before* constructing your typology; you can and should try two or three alternative groupings, such as typologies with various differentiations including maybe four, five, and six types. In the Marienthal study, the mindset types are especially strong because the distinction between the four types is clear, plausible, and comprehensible. If the researchers had attempted to differentiate between eight or more types, the unions and politicians – the main recipients of the study – would likely have had more trouble understanding the results. Conversely, merely including four social milieus in a lifestyle research project would likely be perceived as too simple because current lifestyle studies, such as the Sinus study, include ten or more different types.[11]

In order to determine how to build your types, you must consider your sample size and the dimensionality of your desired attribute space:

- *Monothetic homogenous attribute types* can be created using two or three attributes with relatively few characteristics.
- *Building types by reduction* is much more flexible and can include more features and more characteristics.
- *Polythetic type-building,* however, makes it possible to integrate numerous characteristics and define a truly multi-dimensional attribute space.

With the exception of the homogenous attribute typology, which is virtually self-explanatory, the other two forms of typologies require that the types are described in terms of their position in the attribute space. For typologies that were formed by reduction, creating a list of the attributes that have been combined is usually sufficient, just as we did in the example typology of parental level of education. Characterizing complex polythetic typologies, however, is a little more difficult.

Phase 5: Assign all of the cases to types

An integral part of constructing a typology involves assigning respondents to the selected types. They must be clearly assigned – one respondent cannot be assigned to two or more types simultaneously. After all, it would not make much sense to assign a family in the Marienthal study to both the 'apathetic' and the 'unbroken' mindsets.

So, after you have compared different typologies in the previous step of the analysis and decided which one fits best with the data, you have to focus again on the individual cases. Now you have to decide to which cluster (type) each individual case belongs.

Phase 6: Describe the typology and the individual types

This phase centres on the description of the individual types. In general, you should arrange the types in a suitable order and describe them on the basis of

---

[11]The last version of the Sinus-Milieus was developed in 2011 and differentiates between ten significant clusters (milieus). See www.sinus-institut.de/en/

the attributes you used to create them. Thus, in the Marienthal project, the four different mindset types are presented with as much detail as possible. Particularly meaningful and exemplary statements can be taken from the data. Tabular overviews may increase the clarity of presentation.

Phase 7: Analyse and present results 1: Relationships between types and secondary information

How does a respondent's assignment to a specific type correspond to other themes, categories, or attributes? This phase of the analysis involves examining the empirical data in even greater detail. For example, you could create a table to display thematically coded segments in order to compare them. Topics, attitudes, values, etc. which were not included in the attribute space when the type was created are considered 'secondary information'; although the word 'secondary' by no means implies that they are less important.

Phase 8: Analyse and present results 2: In-depth type-based interpretations of selected cases

The slogan 'Back to the text' applies to the final phase of type-building text analysis. The focus in this phase is on an in-depth interpretation of the newly-constructed typology. The typology provides the backdrop for organizing and interpreting the individual cases. The overviews that display the numerical distributions of types and attributes as well as cases do not speak for themselves and are not sufficient; the types and constellations gain meaning and significance once you refer back to and interpret the individual cases.

What criteria should you use to select the cases for such an in-depth analysis? Because not all of the cases within a qualitative study can be presented in detail in the research report, you have to select a portion of the cases to analyse in more detail. There are two strategies for doing so, as detailed below.

The first option involves creating a *representative case interpretation* based on one single prototypical case per type, which is then presented in detail and deemed representative for all of the respondents that belong to that given type. If you have used a formal method, such as the statistical method of cluster analysis, it will include information about the proximity of each respondent to the centre, which serves as formal criteria for selecting the most suitable cases for in-depth analysis. If you have not used such a formal method, you will have to re-examine the text segments that form the basis of the typology and identify the most suitable case or cases for in-depth analysis. Computer-assisted analysis techniques, such as text retrieval, are very effective aids in this part of the analysis process. In the Marienthal study, this strategy of *representative case interpretation* would mean to select a person that is the best example for the type 'unbroken'. This person and his or her characteristics would then be presented and interpreted. The same would be done for the other three types, the 'resigned', 'the people in despair', and the 'apathetic': Select the most representative persons and describe them in detail. The result is that four (real) people are shown as examples to produce a better understanding of the constructed typology.

The second option for selecting which cases to use in the in-depth analysis involves *constructing a model case* based on a synopsis or montage of the most suitable text segments. This approach is less focused on the individual cases and in many ways similar to Weber's approach of building ideal types. However, because the polythetic types and their position in the attribute space have already been determined via the typological interpretation of the text, they are real, not ideal types, and they represent real individual respondents from the sample. By reviewing relevant text passages, you can determine which cases would be suitable for the given type and include them in the synopsis.

Presentation of Results

Preparing and presenting the results of a type-building text analysis centres on presenting the processes used to build the types, the constructed typology itself, and the individual types. More specifically, you should:

- describe the goal and purpose of building types;
- present the attribute space and the empirical foundation in the data (which categories were used and how they were created);
- present the methods used to construct the typology;
- describe the typology, the individual types, and their differences from other types; and
- include information regarding the frequency of the individual types within the sample as well as your own postulates regarding how to generalize your findings.

Arranging the types in a two-dimensional coordinate system makes it easier to understand a typology, though it is more difficult to do so if the typology contains more than two dimensions. The following example stems from a Wenzler-Cremer study on identity and the life-plans of young German-Indonesian women (Wenzler-Cremer, 2005, p. 336). The typology is arranged in a coordinate system in which the y-axis represents 'belonging to a culture' and the x-axis presents 'use of bicultural resources' (Figure 4.11).

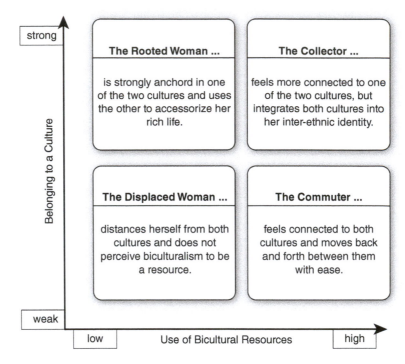

Figure 4.11   Two-Dimensional Representation of Four Types (Wenzler-Cremer, 2005)

The construction of a typology opens up a variety of further analyses you may wish to conduct. For example, you could examine the following options which are arranged clockwise in the diagram:

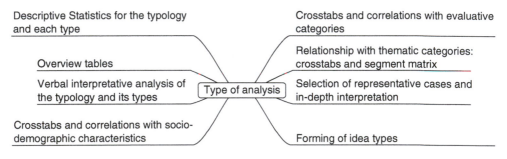

Figure 4.12   Types of Analysis and Presentation of Results in Type-Building Text Analysis

Descriptive statistics: This first option deals with the typology and its types and describes them quantitatively, e.g. the size of the types, number of persons belonging to each type, etc.

Overview tables compare the types and their characteristics in a tabular format. The contents of the tables may be qualitative (verbal description) or quantitative (the distribution of characteristics in numbers and percentages).

Verbal interpretive analysis of the typology and its types: Here the different types are described in words, e.g. what makes a type unique, what are the key differences, etc.

The relationship between types and socio-demographic characteristics, meaning you can examine which combinations of gender, age, level of education, income, etc. are found in which types. Because socio-demographic data are usually standardized, they are especially suitable for statistical analyses.

The relationship between types and evaluative categories: Because evaluative categories present a classification and are based on specific text passages, they can be analysed qualitatively and quantitatively. You can conduct simple and complex statistical analyses and compile the text segments according to the groups you create.

The relationship between types and thematic categories, meaning you can compare the statements that respondents belonging to one type made pertaining to specific thematic categories with the statements of respondents belonging to a different type. You can conduct statistical analyses, such as crosstabs, and verbal-interpretive analyses.

Finally, one can perform in-depth interpretation of selected individuals, which are representative for a particular type.

Or, another option would be that you could probably construct an ideal type of the individuals belonging to the same cluster.

5

Qualitative Text Analysis using Computer Assistance

In this chapter, you will learn about how computer software, particularly QDA software and transcription software can be used in qualitative text analysis. The main topics that will be addressed include:

- Transcribing audio and video data using specialised computer software.
- Making the data anonymous.
- Preparing the data for computer-assisted analysis and importing it to QDA software.
- Performing thematic, evaluative, and type-building qualitative analysis using a computer.
- Using additional analysis options available using QDA software, such as hyperlinks and memos.
- Linking audio and video files to the transcription synchronously.
- Visualizing relationships and dependencies using diagrams, charts, timelines, concept maps, etc.
- Using word-based features such as word frequency, keyword-in-context lists, and dictionary-based automatic coding.

Qualitative social research changed in the mid-1980s with the introduction of computer-assisted analysis using special software programs (Weitzman & Miles, 1995). The first generation of such programs, including The Ethnograph, MAX, Nudist, Atlas.ti, Textbase Alpha, etc. were only known to a small group of pioneers within the field of qualitative research (see Gibbs, 2009; Kelle, Prein, & Bird, 1995; Kuckartz, 2010c; Lewins & Silver, 2007; Tesch, 1992; Weitzman & Miles, 1995). Today, however, things have changed completely: QDA computer programs have been developed and are used fairly standardly in qualitative research. For over two decades, the field of computer-assisted analysis of qualitative data has been considered one of the most innovative fields in social science methodology development. QDA software programs do not prescribe one specific method of analysis, but can be used for many types of data and in a variety of methodological approaches (see Fielding & Lee, 1998; Kelle, 2007a). For example, Creswell (2007, pp. 164–173) describes how QDA software can be used in five different research traditions, including biographical life history, phenomenology, Grounded Theory, ethnography, and case study.

In the following chapter, the capabilities of QDA software will be presented, focusing on systematic qualitative text analysis. The goal of this chapter is to gain an overview of the different possibilities for analysis. Detailed overviews of QDA software's options and features can be found in Kuckartz (2009), Bazeley (2007), Lewins and Silver (2007), and Richards and Richards (1994).

5.1 Managing the Data: Transcribing, Anonymizing, Planning Teamwork

At the beginning of any kind of qualitative text analysis, questions arise regarding how to manage and organize the data. How should we best format the data? How can it be analysed using QDA software? How should we organize, save, and store files and folders? How can we organize and co-ordinate the work within the research team?

If you and your research team have collected the data yourselves, such as using qualitative interviews with audio-recordings, the data must be transcribed first before you can start the analysis. Within social science research, transcription is a fairly complicated matter. Even if a very accurate transcription is not required, the research team must agree on certain rules of transcription.

From data collection to importing the data into the software the following seven steps are performed:

1   Determine a set of transcription rules or choose an established transcription system that is suited for the planned analysis.
2   Transcribe the texts (or part of the texts) on the computer.
3   Proof-read, edit, and modify the transcription, if necessary.
4   Make the transcription anonymous.
5   Format the transcription in such a way that the QDA program can be used optimally.
6   Save and archive the transcription as RTF or DOC/X files.
7   Import these files into the QDA software.

The first three steps are of course only necessary if new data material has been collected and must be transcribed. If the data has already been digitalized, proceed with Step 4 to anonymize, format, and import the existing data into the QDA software.

Rules for Transcription

If possible, when working with qualitative interviews, group discussions, focus groups, and similar forms of data collection, you should work with audio-recordings rather than simply with protocols that should jog your memory. Table 5.1 presents the advantages and disadvantages of using audio-recordings.

Table 5.1 Advantages and Disadvantages of Using Audio-Recordings

Advantages of Audio-Recordings	Disadvantages of Audio-Recordings
Accuracy.	Respondents may feel uncomfortable that everything is being recorded, which may lead to uncertainties or distort the interview.
Direct quotations in research report possible.	Respondents may be less spontaneous because more attention is given to the choice of words.
Immediacy, no distortion via retrospective memory.	Interaction can be disturbed by the recording.
Relaxed interview setting because there is no need to record notes, keywords etc.	*Note*: The potential adverse effects of the audio-recording may weaken as the respondents grow accustomed to the situation as well as the recording devices.
Easier to analyse.	
Critical reflection of the interview techniques and the course of the interview possible.	
Better documentation and controllability, which lead to increased reputation in the scientific community.	

The advantages associated with audio-recordings are obvious, unless you are dealing with particularly sensitive issues which require a very confidential interview setting that would be disturbed by a simultaneous audio-recording. Writing an exact transcription is only possible using an audio- or video-recording, meaning that such recordings are the only way to ensure that you can use direct quotations in later steps of the analysis as well as in the research report.

Audio-recordings are best carried out using digital recording devices, which offer high quality recording capabilities for a relatively low price and can record many hours of interviews. The resulting files can be transferred from the audio-recording device onto a computer where they are then available for transcription. Unfortunately, dictation software programs such as Dragon NaturallySpeaking[1] do not yet offer reliable automatic transcriptions of interviews. Such programs work quite well if they have been trained to one person's voice. However, in order to transcribe interviews using such software, interviewers would have to dictate all of the answers provided by the interviewees again.

The same is true for video-recordings, though researchers usually focus on the audio-recording of the interview. Modern video cameras and transcription software make recording and transcribing interviews fairly easy. The rules for transcription presented in the following sections apply to both audio- and video-recordings.

Determining rules for transcription

Rules for transcription determine how spoken language is transmitted in written form. Some information is always lost in this transmission; thus, the aims and goals of the planned analysis must determine which losses are acceptable and which are not. There are many different transcription systems available (see Kowal & O'Connell, 2004), most of which differ only in whether and how various features are to be included in the transcription, such as intonation and emphasis, volume, drawl, pauses, overlaps between the utterances of different speakers, accents, gestures, facial expressions, and non-verbal expressions such as laughing, coughing, groaning, etc. Furthermore, some characteristics of the interview or interview setting could be relevant for the analysis, such as if someone enters or exits the room or a telephone rings, etc. Whether or not researchers actually transcribe all of these details depends on a study's finances, too, since transcription is very time-consuming and thus involves a considerable expense. Even simple transcription takes approximately five times longer than the time necessary for the interview itself. Moreover, documenting the intonation, dialects, and overlaps of different speakers within a group interview or focus group setting would further increase the costs. However, the cost is not the only decisive factor; it is much more important to determine the degree of accuracy necessary or desired for later steps in the

---

[1]See www.nuance.com.

analysis process. Sometimes, transcribing too precisely can hinder the overall analysis, such as when the text is difficult to read as a result of too many transcribed details pertaining to dialect or other features. A relatively simple transcription system is sufficient for most research projects in social research. Within the framework of an evaluation project, we have developed a set of easy to learn transcription rules.[2] These rules have been expanded based on personal experience as well as suggestions from Dresing, Pehl, and Schmieder (2013), and are presented below.

Rules for Transcription for Computer-Assisted Analysis

1 Transcriptions should be verbatim, not based on sounds or simply contain summaries. Any components of dialects should be translated into the standard language.

2 Language and punctuation should be smoothed slightly to accommodate written standards.

3 Long, clear pauses should be marked by an ellipsis in parentheses (...), with each period representing one second of the pause. For longer pauses, the number of seconds can be indicated by a number within parentheses.

4 Any terms that the respondent emphasized should be underlined.

5 Anything the respondent says loudly should be capitalized.

6 The approving or affirming vocalizations on the part of the interviewer (mhm, aha, etc.) should not be transcribed as long as they do not interrupt the respondent's flow of speech.

7 Any objections that other individuals or respondents make should be indicated in parentheses.

8 Any of the respondent's vocalizations that support or clarify a statement (such as laughing or sighing) should be noted in parentheses.

9 Paragraphs belonging to the interviewer should be designated by 'I' while those belonging to the respondent are denoted by an appropriate abbreviation, such as 'R4', etc.

10 Each conversational contribution should be transcribed as its own paragraph. Changes in speaker are denoted by an empty line (double space). This should improve the readability of the transcription.

(Continued)

---

[2]More details regarding complex transcription rules can be found in Kuckartz (2010a, pp. 38–47).

(Continued)

11 Any disruptions should be listed specifically (e.g. telephone rings).

12 Non-verbal activities on the part of the interviewer as well as the interviewee should be noted in double parentheses, such as ((laughs)), ((sighs)), and the like.

13 Unintelligible or unclear words should be noted as such (unclear).

14 All information that would identify a specific respondent should be made anonymous.

Symbol	Name	Use
[Text]	Brackets	Indicates the start and end points of overlapping speech.
=	Equal Sign	Indicates the break and subsequent continuation of a single utterance.
(# seconds)	Timed Pause	A number in parentheses indicates the time, in seconds, of a pause in speech.
(.)	Micro Pause	A brief pause, usually less than 0.2 seconds.
. or ↓	Period or Down Arrow	Indicates falling pitch or intonation.
? or ↑	Question Mark or Up Arrow	Indicates rising pitch or intonation.
,	Comma	Indicates a temporary rise or fall in intonation.
-	Hyphen	Indicates an abrupt halt or interruption in utterance.
>Text<	Greater than / Less than Symbols	Indicates that the enclosed speech was delivered more rapidly than usual for the speaker.
<Text>	Less than / Greater than Symbols	Indicates that the enclosed speech was delivered more slowly than usual for the speaker.
°	Degree Symbol	Indicates a whisper, reduced volume, or quiet speech.
ALL CAPS	Capitalized Text	Indicates shouted or increased volume speech.
Underline	Underlined Text	Indicates the speaker is emphasizing or stressing the speech.
:::	Colon(s)	Indicates prolongation of a sound.
(hhh)		Audible exhalation.
· or (.hhh)	High Dot	Audible inhalation.
(Text)	Parentheses	Speech which is unclear or in doubt in the transcript.
((*italic text*))	Double Parentheses	Annotation of non-verbal activity.

Figure 5.1 The Jefferson Notation System (1984)[1]

[1]The Jefferson Transcript Notation can be found on Transana's website: http://www.transana.org/support/online-help/team1/transcriptnotation1.html (accessed 20 March 2013)

Dresing, Pehl and Schmieder supplement these rules with instructions for uniform notation which are especially useful within the framework of a research group where multiple researchers are involved in transcribing interviews.

Much more complex transcription systems exist within the framework of linguistic analysis and in conversational research, such as GAT, HIAT and CHAT. Moreover, EXMARaLDA[3] represents a software program for more complex transcriptions. The transcription system developed by the American linguist Gail Jefferson (1984) is particularly popular in the English-speaking realm and is presented in Figure 5.1. Jefferson was one of the founders of Conversational Analysis and was particularly interested in the fine details of conversations and interactions.

Transcribing using a computer

A number of different computer programs are available for transcribing audio and video files. Among them are ExpressScribe, Inqscribe, HyperTranscribe and f4.[4] In general the programs are easy to use and contain all of the functions normally required for transcribing interviews within social research.[5] Like with most media players, you can play, stop, pause, re-start, rewind, and fast-forward as desired. In addition, you can adjust the playback speed as well as the return interval, or the time in seconds that the recording rewinds and resets upon stopping. Using a footswitch or pedal is useful for stopping and starting the recording while transcribing.

The transcription software can insert a time stamp into the transcript, for instance at the beginning or end of a paragraph (when you push the Enter key). This makes it possible to synchronize the text and audio-recording so that you can click on a given time stamp when reading the text in order to play that exact excerpt of the audio-recording. Figure 5.2 shows an excerpt of a transcript that was created in accordance to the presented rules.

In general, the transcripts should be formatted so that they are easy to read on the computer screen in later steps of the analysis process and so that they can utilize various functions within the QDA software programs, particularly

---

[3]See www.exmaralda.org.

[4]For example, ExpressScribe (http://www.nch.com.au/scribe/index.html), f4 (http://www.audiotranskription.de/english/f4.htm), Hypertranscribe (www.researchware.com/products/hypertranscribe.html), InqScribe (www.inqscribe.com), Transcriber (http://trans.source-forge.net/en/presentation.php)

[5]The software programs f4 and f4media as well as f5 (for Macs) are available as free downloads at http://www.audiotranskription.de/english/f4.htm.

R7:	My boyfriend and I have a study group. I mean, I explain everything to him two times and then I understand it better myself. And, yeah, I studied with one of the other students from my statistics group one time, too.
I:	And how do you feel when you are studying? Do you have a positive or negative attitude or feeling towards statistics or (...)?
R7:	I like it a lot. I didn't think that would be the case, but I always liked math, so I think that's why I think it's OK.
I:	And did that change at all over the course of the semester? (R7: Yes!) If so, how so?

Figure 5.2 Excerpt of a Transcript (Interview with Participant 7)

the lexical or word-based search options. Irrespective of the transcription system or transcription program used, it is important that the terms used to identify either the speaker, a specific question from the interview-guide, or a particular section of the survey are maintained throughout the entire text. For example, to identify the interviewer, choose how you would like to abbreviate him or her and use the same abbreviation throughout the entire work, such as 'I', or 'INT' and not interchangeably 'I', 'INT', and even 'Interviewer'. Uniform spelling and referencing are absolutely imperative if you plan to use the lexical search options in QDA software later.

After the transcription is finished, the entire text should be edited and, where necessary, modified before it is imported into the analysis software. It is recommended that interviewers take the time to compare the transcript with the audio-recording one last time.

In qualitative research, the analysis of the interview begins with or even before the transcription: Researchers develop ideas and maybe even hypotheses for analysis during the interview and while listening to the audio-recordings. They keep the interview situation and any particularities in mind and may already mention them to and discuss them with the research team. *All of these thoughts deserve to be recorded*, though not within the transcript itself. Such ideas should be documented in the form of notes and memos that can be saved together with the text and linked to the corresponding passages.

Making the Data Anonymous

Qualitative data usually contains sensitive information that can be used to directly identify respondents; thus, it must be made anonymous. Depending on the type of data, it can be made anonymous during the transcription phase or upon completion of the transcription. If the data set contains a large number of details that need to be made anonymous, it is usually recommended to wait until the transcription is complete. Even if the transcription is completed by a typing service or by office assistants who were not involved in obtaining the data, making the data anonymous during the transcription process is not recommended because it would overwhelm the transcribers.

When making the data anonymous, all of the sensitive data in the form of names, places, dates and the like, must be replaced by pseudo names or abbreviations. They must be changed so that the respondents cannot be directly identified based on the information contained in the transcript. Places can be replaced by more general references such as 'small town' or 'village' and dates can be changed to indicate general time frames, such as 'summer' or 'last winter'. A table should be created to summarize the changes and provide information for decrypting the anonymization, which, of course, must be stored separately from the data itself in order to maintain privacy and confidentiality.

After the data has been edited, formatted, and made anonymous, it should be saved as an RTF or DOC/X file on two different computing systems to ensure that it is backed-up sufficiently. Saving two copies on one hard disc will not be of much assistance if the hard disc crashes.

Organizing Data and Planning Teamwork

Qualitative data is usually quite extensive and can contain hundreds or even thousands of pages of text, which take the form of transcribed interviews, field notes, observation protocols, documents, and more. Before beginning the actual analysis, you should ponder how to organize all of the data. Ask yourself: What data are available for analysis? How large is this dataset? Can I divide it into meaningful groups? Next, determine which options your selected QDA software offers for optimal organizing and structuring the data.

In the case of our example project, in which we interviewed individuals from two different age groups, it makes sense to organize the data into two text groups or folders. This makes it easier to perform separate analyses on the two groups later. Each of the interviews should be treated as an individual text; normally, it is not recommended to organize all interviews together into one file.

Moreover, you must also determine whether your audio files should be archived and made available for occasional use or readily available for frequent use. Audio files are relatively bulky; thus, you must decide if you really need them for the analysis. Keep in mind that exchanging project files via the Internet could be more difficult if any given file contains over a hundred megabytes or even one or more gigabytes, as transferring such files would require more time and may not even be supported by some email servers. In addition, researchers must adhere to laws and standards regarding data protection.

Any standardized data (such as socio-demographic data) that you collected along with your qualitative data should be available throughout the qualitative text analysis process so that you can, for example, analyse a specific group of the respondents. It is advantageous to organize the standardized data (variables) into spreadsheets, using Excel, for example, because Excel files can be imported into the statistic software easily, which makes it easy to conduct statistical analyses (frequency tables, crosstabs, etc.) without having to re-define variables.

Memos that you composed during your first reading of the material or during the transcription process must also be organized. You must decide if you would like to label them as a special kind of text that you can link to the interviews or organize them as memos that belong to a given text or text passage. The latter is advantageous because the memos are always directly associated with the text that they reference and they are easily accessible. Postscripts written by the interviewers or that pertain to the interviews should be organized in a similar manner (see Witzel, 2000, p. 8).

The question of sub-dividing the text into text units or units of meaning goes back to the transcription phase but can only be answered later in the analysis process. If you plan to code the data according to syntactic or semantic aspects in subsequent codings, now is the time to split up the data into logical paragraphs. It is useful to begin a new paragraph for each meaningful unit of text. In primarily interpretative analyses, defining different groups in advance may seem unnecessary; however, the more elements of quantitative content analysis you plan to integrate into your analysis, the more useful these sorts of sub-divisions can be.

In her book *Qualitative Content Analysis in Practice*, Schreier (2012, p. 129) emphasized that the texts must be segmented into units before they can be coded in the analysis. Today's QDA software is so flexible that this restriction is no longer necessary for qualitative text analysis.

When different members of a research team are involved in analysing the data, it is important to think about how to organize and co-ordinate your work as a team. Consider the following questions:

- How will we work together?
- Should all of the team members be able to work on the same text at the same time?
- Shall we assign specific texts to specific members of the team so that each researcher is responsible for specific texts?
- Does the selected QDA software support our form of teamwork? Are there multiple alternatives for working in teams? If so, which is the most fitting for the current analysis?

Another question to address is how much access the different members of your team will have to the data. Should everyone be allowed to make changes to the common database, such as to code text, define or delete codes, or re-structure the category system, when working with the project? In general, teamwork is a complex issue particularly if people are working with the same database at the same time in different places. Moreover, working in teams and exchanging data can be hindered by technical and organizational limitations; research teams should be sure to consider their options from the start.

5.2 Qualitative Text Analysis Using QDA Software

In the following, we will describe how QDA software programs can be used to help build categories as well as how they can be implemented within each of the three methods of qualitative text analysis described in the previous chapter. Because software programs quickly become obsolete and new versions often include changes to menus and interfaces, the following sections will concentrate on the general approach instead of providing specific instructions, such as 'Select item xy from the menu', 'Click here', or 'Double click there'.

Importing Data into the QDA Software

Importing qualitative data into QDA software is a simple process. Depending on the given software, importing files may require little more than simply using the mouse to drag and drop the desired files into the working surface of the chosen program. DOC or DOC/X and RTF files are accepted by most QDA programs; PDF files can only currently[6] be used in their original layout by MAXQDA, NVivo and Atlas.ti. When analysing studies based on interviews, DOC/X or RTF formats are more suitable than PDF because they allow you to add and edit text at any point in the analysis process. This might, for example, be necessary in order to make the text anonymous later in the analysis process. Moreover, only DOC/X or RTF formats allow you to use a synchronous time stamp in the transcription to access the audio and video files.

Some types of texts, such as transcriptions of focus groups, answers to open-ended questions in online surveys, and texts that stem from Internet forums, can be imported into QDA software in a pre-structured format. The software then automatically assigns text passages to main categories and subcategories or, in the case of group discussions or focus groups, to different speakers (see Kuckartz, 2010a, pp. 49–55).

Tools for Working through the Text: Comments, Memos, Highlighting Passages of Text

QDA software programs offer useful support already in the initial phase of working with the text in qualitative data analysis. This begins with numbering

---

[6]As of 1 December 2012.

the paragraphs or lines of a respondent's statements, which can serve as the basis for the discussion within the research team. Moreover, QDA software allows you to search the entire data set for interesting words or phrases and view all of the relevant passages with virtually one click. You can also highlight or change the colour of text passages that you deem especially interesting or important and add your own comments. All of this is possible before the actual analysis begins, i.e. before you build categories, code the text, and start the category-based analysis.

Thus, qualitative data analysis begins, in fact, before the first coding process. If you consider the researchers to be active subjects involved in the research instead of just agents for collecting data, it is easier to understand the entire qualitative research process as a process of data analysis in which, unlike in survey research, there is no strict separation between collecting and analysing the data. If the researcher conducts the interview him or herself, he or she will automatically analyse certain statements according to his or her own previous knowledge as well as the interview question. Glaser and Strauss refer to this as coding because researchers 'code' what they hear, arrange it in their minds and ponder it while considering their own ideas and forming hypotheses regarding the relationships (see Glaser & Strauss, 1998, pp. 107–121). All of this occurs in every stage of the research process, including the early phases of data collection; thus, you should record such ideas and hypotheses immediately, preferably in the form of memos (see Section 3.3). The way that codes and coding schemes are used in qualitative text analysis differs from the style of analysis that is often used in Grounded Theory, where the analytical work is very focused on the development of codes and key codes. Nevertheless, it is recommended that you record your ideas, theoretical considerations, and hypotheses from the start of the analysis process.

The founders of Grounded Theory (Strauss, Glaser, Corbin and others) use the term 'memo' in reference to such notes, annotations, and comments, which play a central role in their analysis. According to the Grounded Theory approach, you should differentiate between different types of memos, including theoretical memos ('theory memos'), memos that note the definitions of the categories and their characteristics or attributes ('code memos'), and memos that contain case summaries ('document memos').

In QDA software, memos can be linked to any kind of object, such as text passages, categories, and sub-categories. It is recommended that you use different symbols to represent different types of memos. Over the course of the analysis process, you can combine individual memos to form larger, integrated memos that serve as building blocks for the research report.

Building Codes and Categories Using the Data

QDA software can be very useful for inductively developing codes and categories directly based on the data. In the Grounded Theory technique of open coding, the codes and concepts are recorded directly in the text: By proceeding through the text line-by-line, according to Strauss and Corbin, you can open up and break up the text (Strauss & Corbin, 1996, p. 45). Much like when working with a pen and paper, you can highlight text passages and assign them a code, a term, or a concept.

The main advantage of using QDA software is that the codes will automatically be recorded into a code system, which can be sorted, systemized, and summarized later in the analysis process. The codes remain linked with the individual text passages so that you can jump back and forth between the analysis and the actual data on which it is based with one click.

Comments, theoretical aspects, and ideas regarding the different dimensions of the codes can be recorded in the form of code memos, which contain detailed descriptions of categories. Figure 5.3 shows an excerpt of an open-coded interview in which the codings are displayed to the left of the text. Notice that a memo has been linked to Paragraph 22, in which the switch from first-person to third-person language is evident: When asked about his or her own behaviour, the respondent answers 'Sure, I would like to' but then switches to the less obligatory third-person and says less concretely, 'You look for an occasion to do so'.

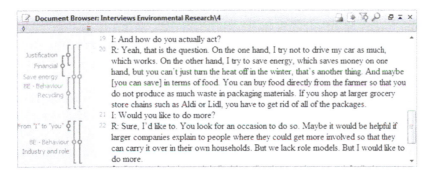

Figure 5.3 Interview Excerpt with Codings Displayed on the Left

Qualitative methods characteristically claim to allow the respondents to speak for themselves – to let them express things in their own words and not simply choose their answers from a number of standard responses. Therefore, their words, concepts, and metaphors are extremely important. QDA software helps you keep track of the respondents' original wording using a feature called 'in-vivo coding', in which the respondents' statements are highlighted and coded and simultaneously recorded as codes within the category system.

For example, one of the respondents in our 'Individual Perception of Climate Change' study referred to what he or she called a 'We-Save-the-World Association'. This term was highlighted and used directly as a category name (see Figure 5.4).

I:	And would you like to do more than you do now?
R29:	Theoretically, yes, but the question is how. And I don't know if I would feel comfortable in some (...) We-Save-the-World Association.
I:	Do you feel a responsibility to address the problems of the 21st century?
R29:	Personally yes, but not globally.
I:	Can you clarify what you mean by that?

Figure 5.4 Excerpt from Interview with R29, Paragraphs 33–37

Building categories is a lengthy process which requires that you go through the data or parts of the data repeatedly. As described in Chapter 3.4, you can also paraphrase, abstract, and summarize particularly meaningful text passages. The process of paraphrasing the text is quite time-consuming, but proves quite helpful, especially for beginners. When using QDA software, it is best to create a table, in which you can enter the paraphrases of the relevant text passages and then reformulate them more generally in order to define the categories.

In a Grounded Theory-oriented approach, codes are formed from the outset with the intention of moving away from the data with the goal of developing a theory. What Strauss, Glaser and Corbin refer to as *coding* (see Strauss & Corbin, 1996, pp. 43–55) refers to the theoretical classification of the data, not simply the assignment to codes. This involves two steps: First anything interesting in the text is coded, meaning that it is given an abstract label. Then, you move to the code level to group the codes and examine the relationships between them.

Using QDA software programs to construct categories for qualitative data analysis has many advantages compared to traditional, manual methods using a pen and paper. This is true for all different kinds of qualitative text analysis, for paraphrasing methods as well as for more abstracting und generalizing approaches that are inspired by the theory-oriented analysis style of Grounded Theory. When using the QDA programs, you stay connected to the original data and are not forced to page through hundreds of pages of text searching for specific text passages. You can easily gain an overview of how frequently certain codes, concepts, and categories appear in the data, and you can find them, summarize them, and create thematic categories for them that can be used in the thematic text analysis. Likewise, you can easily find typical examples to help define the given thematic categories.

For documentation purposes, you can always determine on which text passages a given category is based. Moreover, you can document the different stages of building categories. You can also determine a category's semantic context because all of the text passages that are linked to a given category are summarized in a list.

If you do not wish to assign codes to relevant text passages when you deal with the text for the first time, we recommend that you work with the QDA software programs in two phases: First you mark important paragraphs and then code them in the second step. For instance, MAXQDA allows you to highlight text electronically in different colours. Like when highlighting on paper, you can start by simply highlighting text passages that are important for your research question. Then, you can go back through the data a second time to assign codes to the passages and create categories.

Thematic Text Analysis

The ways in which QDA software can assist in thematic text analysis are presented in Table 5.2. The left column presents the given phase of the thematic analysis and the right column presents the implementation using QDA software.

Table 5.2 Using QDA Software for Thematic Qualitative Text Analysis

Phase	Computer Assistance
Initial work with the text	You can highlight important text passages and code them. You also can automatically search for certain words or phrases. You may write memos and comments and link them to text passages, to the entire text, or to categories. Text passages can be linked together, for example, if they are similar or contradictory, etc. You also may link text passages with external documents to provide a broader context for the analysis.
	You can compose case summaries and save them as memos linked to the text.
Develop main thematic categories	You can select text passages with the mouse and assign codes (or labels). The codes can be grouped or combined into more abstract categories. Descriptions and definitions of categories should be recorded in code memos.
First coding process (using main categories)	You should sequentially work through each text line-by-line and assign your main categories to relevant text passages.

(Continued)

Table 5.2   (Continued)

Phase	Computer Assistance
Compile all of the text passages assigned to the main categories	Using the text retrieval function, all of the text passages that have been assigned to a given main category can be summarized into a list that may be printed or saved as a DOC-file or spreadsheet. Standardized data (such as socio-demographic characteristics) can be used for selecting, grouping, and contrasting the categories.
Inductively define sub-categories based on the data	You can develop sub-categories for each of the main categories directly based on the data. As before, you should record these definitions as code memos and add typical examples to the category descriptions. Then, you can create coding guidelines for the category system that you have constructed.
Second coding process (using the elaborate category system)	You should now go back through all of the text passages that have been coded with the main categories in order to assign them to the constructed sub-categories.
	Modify the case summaries as necessary based on the main categories and sub-categories and record them again as memos.
Analyse and present the results Part 1: Category-based analysis	The text retrieval function allows you to compile the text passages that have been assigned to a category or sub-category and determine the frequency with which each sub-category appears. This allows you to analyse any overlaps between the categories and sub-categories. Selective text retrievals enable you to compare sub-groups of your data.
Analyse and present the results Part 2: Relations, visualizations and tables	Visual representations show the presence and, if desired, the frequency of the thematic categories broken down by text.
	Diagrams present the proximity of categories and sub-categories (and any overlaps between them).
	The thematic progression of an interview can be displayed as 'codeline'. In the case of group discussions, the sequence in which the speakers spoke and the topics of each of their contributions are displayed.
	Concept maps and diagrams visualize the relationships between the categories and present the hypotheses and theories developed during the analysis (e.g. in the form of causal models).
	During the analysis process, you can integrate the memos into the corresponding sections or chapters of the research report.

Table 5.2 shows that QDA software can be integrated into every phase of thematic text analysis to very effectively assist in the analysis, and it is, by no means, a complete list of the capabilities that QDA software programs offer. When it comes to the research report, it is important that you define your framework and determine how you would like to report the results of the analysis and how long you would like your research report to be. For instance,

it may be suitable to allot 60 pages to the results section of a dissertation, but you would only be allotted five to ten pages for an article in a journal or book.

Developing a storyline is quite useful. Starting with the research question that serves as the basis for the research, you can develop the story by introducing the categories that you wish to write about in such a way that they tease the readers' interest. Once you have conceptualized the general structure of the research report, you can adjust the number of pages allocated as necessary, but it is helpful to know what you are aiming for as you begin writing about your analysis of the first category.

In the category-based analysis, retrieving the texts that correspond to the given category or sub-categories serves as the starting point for the writing process.

In computer-assisted qualitative analysis, a text retrieval is a category-based compilation of the text passages that have been coded with the same code. The text passages that the QDA software compiles usually contain information regarding their origin, i.e. information about which text they stem from and where they can be found within the given text. You can view the compiled list of texts on the screen, print it, or export it into other programs for further analysis.

Take, for instance, the category 'The largest problems in the world' in our example project. Let's examine the problems that the respondents indicated as the largest problems in the world today (which we defined as sub-categories). Which problems are named frequently? Which are seldom named? Which problems are frequently named in association with other problems? Which groups of respondents name which problems? Examining a thematic category in detail often leads to the development of additional sub-categories or dimensions. You do not always have to go through the entire data set again in order to differentiate between different dimensions and re-code the relevant text passages. You can also organize the answers in a simple, systemized manner and prepare them for the research report.

QDA software can be particularly useful for condensing and summarizing coded texts. Such techniques are described in detail in Chapter 3. The so-called 'Summary Grid' of the software MAXQDA allows a systematic form of category-based summaries. Figure 5.5 illustrates the work with the Summary Grid. In the left panel you will find the thematic matrix, as described in Chapter 3. The rows of the matrix are formed by the various interviews, and the columns represent the categories. Once you click on a cell in the thematic matrix, the associated coded segments of the person are displayed in the middle pane. In the right pane, the researchers can then write a summary of the coded segments.

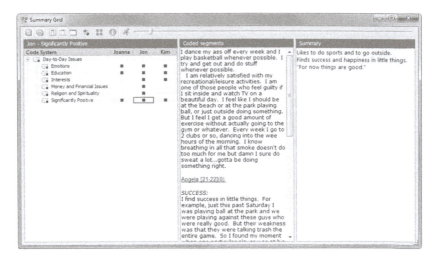

Figure 5.5 Summarizing Coded Segments by Use of the Summary Grid

Evaluative Text Analysis

Evaluative text analysis can be easily implemented based on the thematic coding established within the framework of the thematic text analysis. Since you have already identified all of the text passages that pertain to important topics, you only have to read, classify, and evaluate these passages. If you have not yet identified and coded such relevant passages, you will have to go back through the text and do so. Otherwise, your analysis will not be linked to the original data and it will be difficult to trace back to the data.

The ways in which QDA software can assist in the seven phases of evaluative text analysis are presented in Table 5.3.

In principle, there are two different ways to evaluate cases, e.g. persons, families, institutions, etc. First, you can decide from the start to analyse the cases based on the categories, which requires you to read through the collection of relevant text passages (Phases 3 and 5), determine adequate characteristics based on the definition of each evaluative category, and assign the given respondent an assessment variable or level (for example, sense of responsibility a high level). Or, you can decide to conduct detailed evaluations of every relevant text passage, meaning that you evaluate the level of responsibility expressed in each of the text passages. In this case, the levels 'high', 'moderate', 'low', and 'unable to classify' can be defined as subcategories for the code 'sense of responsibility' and assigned to the appropriate text passages.

Table 5.3 Using QDA Software for Evaluative Qualitative Text Analysis

Phase		Computer Assistance
1	Determine the categories (based on the research question) that should be used as evaluative categories.	Search and retrieval functions make it easy to gain an overview of the data and determine if it is suitable for evaluative text analysis.
2	Identify and code all of the text passages that are relevant to a given evaluative category.	QDA software codes the data quickly and efficiently. You can also compare the codings completed by different coders. Code memos allow you to record and modify category definitions and typical examples.
3	Compile text segments coded with the same category.	You can use the text retrieval function to compile all of the text passages that belong to a given category. The results of the retrieval can be displayed in sequential mode, as a table, and printed.
4	Define levels (values) for the evaluative categories and assign them to the text segments. If necessary, modify the category definition and the number of category values.	Category characteristics can be defined as sub-categories. You can assign text passages to the appropriate sub-category by dragging and dropping them into the appropriate section of the table. You can record dynamic changes to the definitions of characteristics and typical examples using the memo function. By changing the number of levels or characteristics that belong to a category, you can select existing codings and reassign them to fit the revised category system.
5	Code the entire data set. If uncertain how to code a given passage, make note of your considerations.	Using the drag and drop function, you can assign text passages to the appropriate sub-category in the table, which orders the cases sequentially. If uncertain how to code a given passage, use the memo function to document your reasoning.
6	Comprehensive, category-based analysis.	The text retrieval function allows you to compile the text passages that have been assigned to a category or sub-category and determine the frequency with which each sub-category appears. This allows you to analyse any co-occurrences or overlaps between the categories and sub-categories. Selective text retrievals enable you to compare sub-groups. The characteristics can serve as selection criteria of the thematic text analysis.

(Continued)

Table 5.3   (Continued)

Phase		Computer Assistance
7	Create quantitative and qualitative data overviews and crosstabs, and conduct in-depth interpretations of cases	You can create quantitative overviews of the entire data sample, including absolute and relative frequencies of the characteristics within each category, crosstabs of the categories, quantitative comparisons between the different sub-groups, etc.
		Converting the evaluative categories into variables allows you to analyse statistical correlations, for example, in crosstabs.
		For some patterns of characteristics, you can examine the respondents' verbal data in order to conduct in-depth analyses of individual cases.

QDA software allows coders to code independently. After all of the data has been coded, coders can compare their individual codings, discuss any differences in their results, and find a consensual solution. At times, the definitions in the coding guidelines must be modified or made more precise. If coders cannot reach an agreement, they can record their pro and contra arguments in the form of a memo, which can be discussed later with the research team or project management.

After the entire data set has been coded with the evaluative categories in Phase 5, QDA software offers a variety of options for further analysis:

- You can determine the frequencies of the characteristics within each category.
- The characteristics can serve as selection criteria for accessing the statements that respondents made about other topics. For example, you can determine what people with a high level of responsibility say about their sources of information regarding the topic 'climate change'.
- You can transfer all the codings that have been done as a codes-by-cases matrix into statistical analysis programs. This allows you to examine the relationships between different evaluative categories, for example, to question 'What influence does a person's sense of responsibility have?' or 'With which other categories does sense of responsibility correlate?'
- The evaluative categories can be incorporated into crosstabs and visualizations.

If you coded by smaller sections and defined the characteristics of the evaluative categories as sub-categories, you will have to aggregate your codings at the case level. You may have evaluated several relevant text passages with different values for a given participant: For instance, some text passages show that a person feels very responsible towards climate change, other text passages show only moderate responsibility. In some QDA programs, these evaluations can be automatically converted into categorical variables. Thus, the variable with the name 'sense of responsibility' automatically contains the value of the most frequently assigned characteristic or level for each respondent. The most frequently assigned characteristic or level may be unclear because two or more sub-categories have the same frequency, in which case the value is set to 'undecided'. As a result, the coders must re-examine the given text passages and assign an adequate value manually. Once all of the texts in the data sample have been coded, you can transfer the variables into other statistical programs, such as Excel, SPSS, SYSTAT, etc. for further analysis.

After exporting the matrix of codings, you can calculate frequency distributions and percentages, which provide an overview of how many of the respondents were classified with a 'high' or 'low' sense of responsibility. If desired, you can create graphical representations, such as pie charts and bar graphs.

Then, you can also create crosstabs, for instance, to compare sense of responsibility with level of education. The variable values can be used within the QDA software to refer to coded text passages that belong to other categories. You can, for example, examine how the respondents with a low sense of responsibility define the world's largest problems and compare them to the respondents with a high sense of responsibility.

Type-Building Text Analysis

Type-building text analysis can also be very well supported by QDA software. In fact, QDA software has even made it possible for the first time to construct types and typologies for qualitative data analysis in a methodical manner, so that the process of constructing types is totally transparent. The ways in which QDA software can assist in building types for qualitative text analysis are presented in Table 5.4.

It is very easy to construct typologies based on the combinations of attributes and to construct ideal types using QDA software because the software allows you to select the appropriate attributes and types and combine them with just a few mouse clicks. Categories and sub-categories can be converted into case variables by establishing a data matrix and recording if and how frequently a given category has been assigned to a given respondent. If you have already conducted an evaluative text analysis, the appropriate assignments have already been saved as case variables. Now you can examine the individual groups separately or compare them with each other. In addition, you can export these case variables into other statistical programs in order to create crosstabs, which can then serve as the basis for building types via the method of reduction.

Type-building analysis benefits even more from the use of QDA software when you rely on statistical approaches – such as cluster analysis, factor analysis, and correspondence analysis – to help to construct the types. This is particularly useful when you work with a large number of cases and/or you

Table 5.4   Using QDA Software for Type-Building Qualitative Text Analysis

	Phase	Computer Assistance
1	Select the relevant dimensions for the typology and determine the attribute space based on the research question or theory.	Search and retrieval functions make it easy to gain an overview of the data and determine if it is suitable for type-building text analysis.
2	Select the data to be used to build the types, either thematic categories and/or evaluative categories. If necessary, code the data for the type-building analysis.	Determine if sufficient information is available regarding the categories, sub-categories, and codings and whether any of the thematic or evaluative codes should be summarized.
3	*Code or re-code the data.* If any attributes have not been coded, you must first conduct a thematic or evaluative coding.	Use the appropriate functionality of the QDA software to code or summarize the different categories.
4	*Determine the method you would like to use to construct the types and typology:*	In some cases, it may be necessary to experiment with different groupings.
	a) Create types with homogeneous attributes by combining them.	Combine categories and build types.
	b) Construct types via reduction.	Combine different categories and construct suitable types by reasonably reducing the attribute space. Combine different attribute combinations into groups.
	c) Construct types with heterogeneous attributes (polythetic types).	Choose between several approaches for constructing types with heterogeneous attributes: a) Group the given case summaries into homogenous clusters. b) Export the data within the attribute space into a statistical software program and conduct appropriate statistical analyses such as cluster analysis or factor analysis. Then map each individual to a cluster.
5	*Assign all of the cases within your study to the constructed types.*	You can create the typology as a new variable or category in the QDA software by assigning it a label or code, such as 'mentality towards the environment'.
		Define the different types you create as characteristics. For example, the typology 'mentality towards the environment' contains the four types 'rhetoricians', 'ignoramuses', 'consistent protectors', and 'uncommitted protectors'.
		Assign each respondent to one of the four types.
6	*Describe the typology and the constructed types.* Describe each type in detail and note how they relate to each other.	Using a text retrieval, compile the text passages that have been coded with the thematic and evaluative categories that are contained in the attribute space that was used to create the types. Save the resulting text as a memo for each type.

	Phase	Computer Assistance
7	*Analyse the relationships between the types and secondary information.*	In this phase, you should conduct statistical as well as qualitative analyses. Using correlations, crosstabs, and variance analyses, you can, for instance, examine the relationships between the types and socio-demographic variables. Using a profile matrix, you can compile and compare the statements respondents made regarding given topics according to their types.
8	*Conduct in-depth type-based analyses of cases:* Interpret representative cases or construct ideal types based on cases belonging to the same type.	The types serve as selection criteria for determining which verbal data to interpret in greater detail. Present, compare, and interpret individual cases. In some cases, you may have to construct (synthesize) an ideal type by compiling the statements of different respondents within the given type.

are working with an attribute space that contains a huge number of attributes. After exporting the matrix of the attributes to be used to construct the types into a statistical software program, you can construct natural typologies using cluster analysis methods. The method assigns the respondents to types, which can then be imported back into the QDA software for the next phase of the analysis.

Even though constructing types relies on case summaries, the QDA software can be useful. In this case, you can start with the case summaries and manually group them into as homogenous groups as possible according to their similarities. This can be done without computer assistance; however, you can still rely on the computer software to present your results, such as by creating diagrams to visualize the types and the respondents that have been assigned to them.

5.3 Advanced Analysis Using QDA Software

Qualitative text analysis, as described above, is not limited to developing categories, coding, and conducting category-based analyses; it also involves examining and working through the texts extensively. QDA software supports this exploration process. The programs offer a toolbox full of useful features and procedures that can each be used creatively as well as usefully combined with others. Describing all of the available tools and their features goes beyond the scope of this book; thus, I will present a brief outline of the functions that go beyond building categories and coding data and are especially useful for qualitative text analysis.

Integrating Multimedia Functionality

Modern QDA software enables users to use multimedia features in qualitative analysis, which means that audio and video files can be synchronized with the transcription and used in the analysis. Since the late 1960s, researchers have been relying on audio-recordings rather than simply taking notes (key words or shorthand) during interviews. When such recordings were done on cassette tapes, transcribing and analysing the recordings was difficult because researchers could only fast-forward the analogue recordings to a certain point when playing them. Everything changed, however, with the advent of digital recording devices, which enable researchers to play nearly any part of the recording virtually without a time delay, which makes it possible to synchronize the recording and the transcription.

In general, it is better to work with the transcripts rather than the audio-recording when analysing the data because transcripts are much easier to handle. For example, you can search for a specific segment of an interview text at lightning speed while it would take much longer to find the same spot in the audio file and listen to it. However, integrating the multimedia functions offers many advantages. You can always access the original recording, which is particularly advantageous if you would like to take para-verbal characteristics into account and pay attention to pitch, delays, volume, and the like. The same applies to video-recordings, which provide even more insight into the research situation and how the data was processed.

Theoretically, this new technology, to have the audio file and the transcript in parallel, allows researchers to omit seemingly unimportant sections of an interview from the transcript since they can always go back and listen to them again, if necessary. The transcription must contain time stamps so that you can directly access the original recording. Some programs work in the opposite direction: When you play the audio file, the transcription appears like subtitles. This can be particularly useful when verifying the accuracy of a transcription.

Integrating multimedia features also involves linking pictures, graphs, and more to the texts. This allows you to present people or groups as well as places, which can increase the clarity of field research.

However, these new possibilities are accompanied by some quite serious problems. One of them is the problem of anonymity. This has always been a problem in qualitative research that should not be under-estimated. Due to the new technology, the problem has increased dramatically. In fact, it is almost impossible to make qualitative data that includes audio and video anonymous:

Voice and video-recordings are difficult to edit in such a way that the respondent's privacy is protected. Secondary analysis of this data is also problematic, as even if respondents provide written consent, researchers have to ask themselves if it is really necessary for the data to be circulating for decades.

Hyperlinks, External Links, and Linking Texts

In QDA software, you can also use hyperlinks, which are, generally speaking, electronic cross-references between two points. If you click on the starting point, you can jump to the destination. This technology is well known through the Internet.

Hyperlinks can also be used as an additional tool in qualitative text analysis to link passages together, both if they stem from one text or from different texts within the research project. This enables you to better understand the data independent of the categories and the coding process. Creating links in QDA software is quite simple: Select the text passages that will serve as your starting point and your destination, creating a permanent link between the two. Links in QDA software appear like those in conventional Internet browsers: If you click on the link, you will jump to the destination. If you click again, you will jump back to the starting point.

Using hyperlinks, you can create a network within your research project that makes it possible to navigate the data independently of the categories. Moreover, you can also use external links to link given text passages with external files, such as photos, audio files, videos, and more. You can use geographical reference tools such as Google Earth[7] in combination with QDA software to gain a new understanding of social objects by examining their co-ordinates, which can be included in the qualitative text analysis. This makes it possible to link any text passages with any desired geographical reference so that you can view the location on the globe that you are examining at any point during the analysis.

Geographical references provide valuable background information for systematic qualitative text analysis. For instance, within the framework of her research on risks, Fielding analysed whether the respondents' assessed risk of flooding and other dangers associated with the climate are connected to where the respondents live (see J. Fielding, 2008). Thus, objective dangers, such as proximity to rivers, elevation of the apartment or house, etc. are related to how the respondents subjectively perceive the threat.

Visualizations

In many scientific disciplines, visualizations are a standard part of an analysis and are used to assist in the diagnosis and analysis as well as the

---

[7]See www.google.com/earth/index.html.

presentation of results. Medical or climate research would not be the same without images and in a variety of disciplines statistical approaches would not be the same without suitable graphs and diagrams of causal models. The idea of using diagrams, tables, and other visualizations within the framework of qualitative data analysis is not new; nearly two decades ago the proponents of Grounded Theory used diagrams to present their concepts (see Strauss, 1991, pp. 238–273; Strauss & Corbin, 1996, pp. 169–192) and Miles and Huberman wrote their comprehensive book *Qualitative Data Analysis: An Expanded Sourcebook* in 1995, which presents visualization techniques in detail and is still very much worth reading because the authors draw attention to different forms of data presentation (see Kuckartz, 2010a, p. 178).

The following describe three of the various visualization techniques available in QDA software for presenting the results of a text analysis:

a) Visualizations that present the thematic progression of an interview.
b) Visualizations of the categories within each interview.
c) Case-based concept maps.

a) Visuals that present the thematic progression of an interview

Visualizing the structure and thematic progression of an interview is particularly interesting in thematic qualitative analysis. The more open the interview is, the more interesting the visualization will be. Likewise, if you rely on an interview-guide and follow a strict sequence of topics in the interview, the visualization will not be as interesting.

Diagrams, such as the one presented in Figure 5.6 which shows how a group discussion progressed, are particularly useful in analysing focus groups,

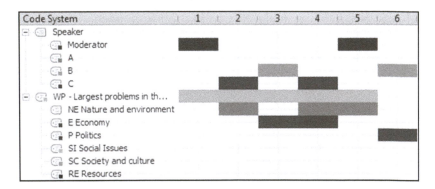

Figure 5.6 Visualization of How a Group Discussion Progressed

providing that each speaker is coded. The diagram shows which of the speakers (here abbreviated as A, B, C) participated in the discussion when and what topics they discussed. Figure 5.6 [8] presents the first six paragraphs of the transcript of a group discussion. After an introduction on the part of the Moderator, Speakers C, B, and then C continue the discussion. The Moderator introduced the topic 'Largest problems in the world' rather generally at first; Speaker C touched on aspects related to 'Nature and the environment'; Speaker B focused on the 'economy' in connection with 'Nature and the environment', which Speaker C continued in Paragraph 4. Then, the Moderator made a reference to 'Nature and the environment' in Paragraph 5 before Speaker C shifted the discussion to address the 'Politics' involved.

b) Visualization of the categories within each interview or case

The concept of the profile matrix, particularly the thematic matrix, which is presented in Chapter 3, is central to qualitative text analysis. A thematic matrix allows you to present cases and categories two-dimensionally. Creating visualizations of the codings increases their potential for analysis because in one glance you can see which categories have been assigned to which interviews. If applicable, you can also visualize how frequently each category has been assigned. Figure 5.7 presents this kind of visualization.[9] You can easily

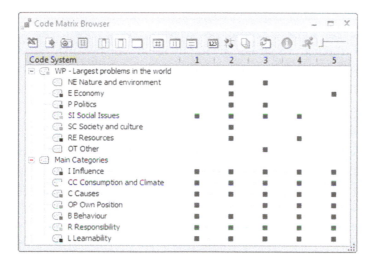

Figure 5.7 Visual Representation of Interviews and Their Assigned Categories

---

[8]This figure was created using the 'Codeline' function in MAXQDA.

[9]This figure was created using the 'Code Matrix Browser' in MAXQDA.

compare texts by arranging them side-by-side – double-clicking on one of the nodes within the thematic matrix displays all of the text passages within the given text that have been coded with this category.

The columns in the figure above display the cases (here Interviews 1 through 5) while the rows correspond to the categories and sub-categories. If you select the corresponding function of the software, it can be seen the size of the symbols shows how often each category was assigned to an interview.

c) Case-based concept maps

Concept maps allow you to examine the relationships between the categories, sub-categories, and cases within a data sample. For example, you can arrange all of the categories that have been assigned to a given interview in such a map, and the categories, in turn, are linked to the appropriate passages in the text. These kinds of visualizations make it possible to determine which categories have been assigned to a given interview in just one glance. Moreover, by clicking on the symbol of a text passage, you can jump right to the underlying data. Concept maps are useful in qualitative text analysis for two main reasons: First, they are especially suitable for presenting the results, such as for presenting the background information as part of an in-depth interpretation of individual cases. Second, they can be used as a diagnostic tool for the actual text analysis and work with the text.

Geographical links can also be inserted into concept maps so that if you click on the text symbol, a geographical information program like Google Earth or Microsoft Virtual Earth will display exactly where the respondent lives.

Word-based Techniques of Analysis

Taking a closer look at words, sentences, and language in general are very important for qualitative data analysis. Thus, it makes sense to also use the word-based analysis capabilities of QDA software programs for qualitative text analysis. As presented in Chapter 2, the classical quantitative content analysis of the 1940s has evolved to include a variety of computer-assisted possibilities for quantitative content analysis that are word-based and process automatic codings on the basis of a dictionary. These word-based techniques can also be used heuristically within qualitative text analysis. Two computer-assisted analysis techniques in particular can be used to supplement qualitative text analysis, namely word frequency counts that display keywords in context as well as dictionary-based word searches and subsequent automatic coding.

a) Word frequency and keywords in context lists

Going through a text sequentially to list all of the words alphabetically and count their frequencies can be quite useful in qualitative text analysis, particularly if you wish to compare selected texts or groups of texts. Computer programs that assist in quantitative content analysis[10] allow you to exclude insignificant words, such as articles and conjunctions, from the analysis by adding them to so-called 'stop lists' or 'exclusion lists'.

Word frequency lists can provide insight into the words that appear most frequently in the text as well as words that are seldom mentioned or words that you would not have expected to find within the given context. Because qualitative research aims to let people express themselves in their own words, it can be interesting to examine linguistic aspects of the interviews. It can be particularly interesting to examine keywords in context and track the use of certain terms in all of or a selected group of the interviews. The resulting lists present the selected terms and the context in which they appear in the texts.

b) Dictionary-based word searches and automatic coding

The technique of creating dictionaries with categories and search terms and using them to code automatically, stems from computer-assisted quantitative content analysis (Krippendorff, 2004, pp. 281–289). The dictionary contains all of the categories as well as search terms that may appear in the text and serve as indicators for the respective categories. For example, if you define the category 'craftsmanship' and compile a corresponding dictionary, you may include professions such as 'shoemaker', 'carpenter', 'wood carver', etc. Then, the passages in which any of the search words appear would be automatically coded and assigned to the category 'craftsmanship'. Ambiguous terms may not be coded correctly using this type of dictionary-based analysis; therefore it may be necessary to re-examine the context of the affected search terms. In our example, both 'Shoemaker' and 'Carpenter' could denote the last names of respondents rather than their professions; thus, coding them to the 'craftsmanship' category may not be appropriate. A simple examination of the context in which the search words appear should clarify such ambiguities.

Dictionary-based coding is a method for reliably analysing a very large amount of data. You can conduct very efficient searches and access the corresponding text passages directly, if necessary. This type of analysis and coding forms a good basis for subsequent statistical analyses, but it can also simply

---

[10]For example, Wordstat (see www.provalisresearch.com/wordstat/Wordstat.html) and MAXDictio (see www.maxqda.com/products).

be used to explore heuristically and make qualitative researchers aware of specific words or word combinations and the passages in which they appear. Dictionary-based content analysis is different than the other text analysis approaches presented in this book because it is an automatic approach, which means that the coding is done by a computer rather than people. Thus, some research questions can be answered very quickly. For example, we conducted a dictionary-based analysis of statements that students made regarding the proposed increases to tuition, which were approximately half of a page long. We were able to identify the different aspects and topics that the students named very quickly if they addressed *social concerns* or *social inequality*, if they thought that the *quality of their studies would be improved* by increased tuition and fees, or if they named *legal aspects*, such as the argument that the German constitution guarantees every individual's right to an education and that imposing additional fees would be illegal. Using the word frequency lists, the terms were assigned to categories within the dictionary and the statements were coded automatically. Then, it was easy to test our hypotheses, such as 'Students connect the issues surrounding increased tuition and fees more frequently with social inequality than with any improvements in the quality of their studies' or 'If a student names social aspects, he or she also names legal aspects'.

Since word-based analyses are limited to single words or phrases and cannot decipher the ambiguity of words, they are limited when it comes to complex research questions. However, such techniques may sometimes supplement qualitative text analysis. They provide a different perspective of the data, draw attention to individual words, and thus allow additional forms of analysis that can help researchers to discover relationships within the data that may not have been visible before. Furthermore, word-based analyses are not very time or labour intensive because they can be conducted on the data without further preparation.

6

Quality Standards, Research Report, and Documentation

In this chapter, you will discover more about:

- Quality standards within qualitative research.
- Internal standards of quality, such as reliability, credibility, and authenticity.
- External standards of quality, such as transferability and adjustability.
- How to compose the research report.
- How to use citations.
- How to document a qualitative text analysis.

How can you distinguish between a good and a poor qualitative text analysis? What standards can be created? How should you plan and structure your research report? What should you document in your research report and what information should be placed in the appendix of the report? How should you cite quotations directly from the data?

This chapter addresses practical questions like those mentioned above, especially within the framework of a Master's thesis or dissertation.

6.1 Quality Standards within Qualitative Text Analysis

We cannot discuss quality standards within qualitative text analysis without considering the importance of standards in qualitative research. Thus, the first question is: What standards generally apply to qualitative research? Do these standards differ from the classical standards of objectivity, reliability, and

Table 6.1 Quality Standards within Quantitative and Qualitative Research

Quality Standards within Quantitative Research	New Quality Standards within Qualitative Research (according to Miles and Huberman)
Objectivity	Conformability
Reliability	Reliability, dependability, auditability
Internal Validity	Credibility and authenticity
External Validity	Transferability and adjustability

validity that have long been recognized in quantitative research? Discussions related to the standards within qualitative research date back to the 1980s and have been very controversial at times (see Flick, 2007a, pp. 487–510; 2009; Guba & Lincoln, 1985; Kirk & Miller, 1986; Spencer, Ritchie, Lewis, & Dillon, 2003; Steinke, 2004). In the 1990s, Miles and Huberman compared classical quality standards with new standards for qualitative research (1995) (see Figure 6.1).

Ultimately, formulating quality standards will always be in reference to epistemological assumptions or to one's world-view, as Creswell and Plano Clark (2011) note. The discussion regarding standards in qualitative research is complex and multi-faceted; however, we will not address it any further here. The pragmatic views of Creswell (2009), Seale (1999b), Flick (2006) and others, are plausible because they attempt to find a new way to determine standards rather than simply blindly rejecting or accepting the classical standards of quality. Their perspective encourages researchers to reformulate quality standards that are relevant to research institutions and can be used to analyse research proposals. Seale and Hammersley's *subtle realism* (see Seale, 1999a, p. 469) serves as the basis for the following observations on the subject of quality standards within qualitative text analysis. Their observations are based on three premises: First, the validity of knowledge cannot be determined with certainty because assumptions can only be judged according to plausibility and credibility. Second, phenomena exist independent of our assumptions about them, although our assumptions can be more or less fitting. Third, reality is accessible from several perspectives we have on the phenomena. Research aims to present reality, not to reproduce it. In empirical qualitative research, the main question is how well the researchers' representations are founded in the data.

In the following, we will discuss quality standards for qualitative text analysis. It seems useful to distinguish between *internal standards of quality*, i.e. authenticity and credibility, and *external standards of quality*, i.e. how well you can transfer and generalize a study. The terms internal and external standards of quality refer intentionally to the terms internal and external validity, which stem from the classical hypothetical-deductive research paradigm. These terms demonstrate that the classical standards cannot simply be transferred over to qualitative research; rather, they have to be modified and extended in order to take the procedural nature of qualitative research into account (see Flick, 2009, pp. 373–375). Formulating the internal standards of quality is a primary goal of using systematic text analysis as a method for analysing qualitative data, while transferring and generalizing the study depends more on the structure of the entire study – its design as well as the methods used for sampling. Similar to the classical quality standards of internal and external validity, internal quality is considered necessary for a study's external quality.

Internal quality of a study: Credibility and authenticity

The quality standards credibility and authenticity not only apply to the approach used for qualitative text analysis, but they are regarded as quality standards for the entire research project. In fact, the quality of the data often only becomes clear during the analysis. Did the interviews achieve authenticity and depth? Did you conduct the interviews according to the rules laid out for the given type of interview? Are the interviewee's answers consistent and credible? Is the structure of the interview appropriate?

The following check list contains key questions used to evaluate the internal quality of a study:

- How were the data recorded? Using audio- or video-recordings, for example?
- Did you follow rules for transcription? Will you disclose these rules?
- What did the transcription process entail?
- Who completed the transcription? The researchers? Or others?
- Did you use specialized transcription software?
- Was it possible to synchronize the audio-recording with the transcription?
- Did you adhere to the rules for transcription and does the written transcript correspond to what was actually said?

The following questions are important for implementing the qualitative text analysis:

- Is the selected method of text analysis appropriate for the research question?
- How do you justify your choice of method?
- Did you implement the selected method correctly?
- Did you complete the text analysis using computer assistance?
- Was the data coded by multiple independent coders?
- How did you achieve consistency in the codings? How did you address any inconsistencies?
- Is the category system coherent?
- Are the categories and sub-categories well structured?
- How precise are the category definitions?
- Did you include typical examples for the categories?

- Does the qualitative analysis take all of the data into account?
- How often did you process the data in order to determine the final codings?
- Have you considered any unusual or abnormal cases? How have you drawn attention to them and analysed them?
- Did you compose memos during the analysis? When? What do they look like?
- Have you included original quotes from the data in your research report? How did you select them? Did you select them according to their plausibility or have you also included counter examples and contradictions?
- Can you justify your conclusions based on the data?

After all, it is crucial – for researchers and evaluators alike – that you disclose the method you used for text analysis and reflect upon it. If you use QDA software, your evaluators can easily understand your category system, how detailed the categories are, how reliably the text passages have been assigned to them, and the level of reflection you have demonstrated in your memos.

External standards of quality: Ability to transfer and generalize results

Even if you can answer all of the questions in the checklists above and the internal quality of your study is excellent, it is not necessarily easy to transfer or generalize the results. How can you ensure that the results of your analysis are meaningful beyond the scope of your study, i.e. they are not only valid in particular situations, but can be *generalized* to apply to other situations and places? This question is not directly related to the quality standards of qualitative text analysis, thus, we would merely like to provide a few references for further reading. Flick (2009, p. 26) considers transferring and generalizing your results to be one of the major goals of qualitative research and notes that you should specifically determine the degree to which you would like to generalize your results. In quantitative research, random sampling (in some cases only quota sampling) of a large number of respondents and subsequent statistical inferences ensure that results can be generalized. However, it should be critically noted that because of constantly declining response rates in survey research, simple statistical inferences are increasingly tainted. Qualitative research cannot rely on the same methods for generalizing the results because qualitative research usually involves smaller samples. However, in qualitative research, you can carefully select a number of cases that include the maximum and minimum number of contrasts, much like theoretical sampling aims to do in the Grounded Theory approach.

Ultimately, you should reflect on how transferrable your research is to the external context of the specific research question at hand. According to Flick, there are steps that can help you determine the transferability of your research and results (2009, p. 276).

Moreover, there are a variety of strategies that can be used to generalize empirical results, including:

- *Peer debriefing* – regular meetings and regular exchanges with competent individuals outside of the research team. These experts examine the approach and the initial results and draw attention to any phenomena or facts that may have been overlooked.
- *Member checking* – discussion of the results with the respondents themselves in order to gain qualified feedback (communicative validation) regarding the research results.
- *Extended stay in the field* – Staying in or returning to the field can help to eliminate premature diagnoses and false conclusions when analysing the data.
- *Triangulation or use of mixed methods* – By using the techniques of triangulation and by combining different research methods (see Denzin, 1978; Flick, 2007b; Kelle, 2007b; Kuckartz, 2009), you can gain diverse perspectives of the research subject as well as additional possibilities for generalizing your work and results.

6.2 Research Report and Documentation

A common misconception is that you cannot record the results until you have reached a certain point towards the end of the research process. This is simply not true: You should write continuously throughout the entire research process and particularly throughout the entire data analysis process. Doing so enables you to accumulate a good deal of information that you can use to write your final research report, which simply constitutes the last stage of this continuous writing process.

The actual results of your study should be included at the end of the research report since, as quoted by a doctoral student at the beginning of this book, 'We want to report results'. As you aim to integrate the different fragments of important information that have surfaced during the analysis, ask yourself: *What is my research question? Whatever I include in the report should answer this question, as it indicates how relevant and how useful the information is in practice or for further research.*

Everything that you have written in the course of the analysis forms the basis for the research report, including:

- Memos that you have written.
- Category descriptions including typical examples.
- Case summaries.
- Excerpts from the literature or reviews.

- Presentations and articles that you may have written over the course of the research project.
- Graphical models and diagrams.
- Visualizations, such as code correspondences.
- Project diary or journal.

Thus, when you start writing the research report, you have a sort of inventory of everything that you have already produced over the course of the research process. If you are working in a team, gaining an overview of this inventory may prove to be a time-consuming task; however, it will also reveal any gaps or areas that require additional preparation. A good amount of literature has been published that provides instructions for writing research papers; thus, we will not list them here. As various authors correctly point out, not all researchers rely on the same writing process or structure. However, you should start with an outline, which could be based on the following general structure:

1 Introduction
2 Explanation of the research question and presentation of any hypotheses and theories on which it is based (if you have formulated hypotheses or your research is based on specific theories)
3 Research methods
4 Results of your research
5 Conclusions

Other important differentiations arise on their own. For example, the methods used to collect data, the type and rules for transcription, and the steps in the qualitative text analysis process will be described in the methods chapter. You can emphasize different elements of your project depending on whether you are writing an academic thesis, a research project funded by a third-party, or an evaluation. Naturally, you may have to adhere to certain forms more rigidly and fulfil specific and detailed requirements in the methods sections of academic theses than in other types of papers. In evaluations, the results, the assessments carried out by the evaluators, and their consequences are usually of primary importance.

When writing the research report in qualitative research, researchers often encounter a phenomenon that Huberman and Miles (1994) refer to as 'data overload': When you have collected so much interesting data, it can be difficult to see the forest for the trees, so to speak. Thus, it can be difficult to select the results and the underlying data: What should you report and what should you omit from the report? Why should you include this case summary and not that one? Why are you focusing on a given category?

Unfortunately, researchers often use up most of their time and energy on transcribing and coding the data. These first few steps of the analysis process can understandably consume large amounts of time, which means that researchers lack the time and energy necessary to conduct complex analyses and compose their research report. We recommend keeping the entire research process in mind, allotting sufficient time for writing and recording your results after you have completed the analysis, and – as mentioned above – thinking about what you would like to write throughout the entire analysis.

While writing, you may worry that your results may have repercussions on the field that you have researched. It is essential that you anticipate these potential effects and include them in your report. This is especially true for evaluations. The Standards for Evaluations, originally developed by the Joint Committee on Standards for Educational Evaluation (JCSEE, see Yarbrough, Shulha, Hopson, & Caruthers, 2011) emphasize the need for fairness:

> **P4 Clarity and Fairness** Evaluations should be understandable and fair in addressing stakeholder needs and purposes. [1]

You should take such standards into account when writing a text and consult the client and stakeholders before finalizing your report, if necessary.

Quotes from the Original Data

Quantitative researchers often feel compelled to present their findings as numbers in the form of percentages, coefficients, correlations, etc. in order to make them more visible to the recipients of their work. Similarly, qualitative researchers often feel compelled to *show* the results of their analysis in the form of verbal data. Wanting to quote passages from the open interviews, for example, is perfectly natural and there is no reason not to include quotes in your research report. Every quote must be labelled as such, omissions must be noted, and researchers should not add emphasis. Like other quotations from other sources, all quotes should contain information regarding their source, including the interview name and paragraph or line number. For example, (R07: 14) and (Ms. Stone: 311–315) represent valid citations with source information. The first example includes an abbreviated interview name and paragraph number and the second example contains a pseudo interviewee name and line numbers.

Quotations should be used sparingly; they should not comprise more than a third or a fourth of the results section, even in a thesis. Reproducing authentic 'sound bites' may seem attractive, but it gives the scholarly paper or thesis a non-analytic character, which should be avoided.

Be aware of selective plausibility, i.e. using original quotations to justify each analytical finding. It can be tempting to do so, but it will likely make your readers suspicious. Thus, you should present contradictory statements in the research report and report a broad spectrum of answers using quotations.

---

[1]See the program evaluation standards on the website of the American Evaluation Association www.eval.org/EvaluationDocuments/progeval.html (accessed 20 March 2013).

Documentation

What should you document and in what form, for example, in an academic thesis? What information must be kept confidential? What should your evaluators be able to understand and verify, if desired?

In the methods section of your actual research report, you should describe the selected method of text analysis clearly and present the categories that were central to the analysis. However, the following elements should be included in the appendix of a thesis or research report:

- Written documents that are important to the study, such as letters.
- Transcription rules and references to relevant standards (which can also be included directly in the text).
- The interview guideline (if applicable).
- The accompanying questionnaire if you have used one.
- Information regarding the length of the individual interviews or at least the average duration and the range of the lengths of the interviews.
- One or more transcripts that serve as examples of the data collected and the type of transcription, if requested by the evaluators.

Moreover, you should include the following data on CD-ROM (if the evaluators would like it):

- Transcripts of the original data in a standard format (DOC, DOCX, RTF, or PDF).
- The final version of the project file if QDA software was used in the analysis.

7

Concluding Remarks

When compared with other methods for qualitative data analysis, systematic qualitative text analysis has many strengths:

- It allows you to conduct a methodically controlled, understandable, and reproducible analysis.
- It is a collection of scientific techniques that can be clearly described and mastered.
- It offers a broad spectrum of different approaches, each of which is suitable in situations and with different requirements.
- It can analyse all of the collected data or the data that has been selected for secondary analysis.
- It is conducive to working in teams of competent researchers.
- It becomes increasingly reliable when implemented by multiple coders.
- It connects a hermeneutical understanding of the text with rule-governed coding.
- It allows computer-assisted analysis.
- It can process a large amount of text, if necessary.
- It forces researchers to develop a category system that includes detailed definitions and typical examples.
- It is a systematic approach that avoids anecdotalism and the suggestion of individual cases.
- It can be conceptualized as a very open and explorative approach, such as in the form of a thematic analysis in which categories are constructed inductively. However, it can also be conceptualized as an approach that is based on hypotheses and pre-determined categories, which means that it is also a theory-driven approach.
- It avoids premature quantification (unlike quantitative content analysis).

Qualitative text analysis is already used in many countries of the world by many researchers in many disciplines, including sociology, pedagogy, political science, psychology, anthropology, social work, education, and health research. In some respects, it is still in its early phases. For example, only recently has a discussion begun which is focused on the importance of ensuring intercoder agreement. However, we can be fairly sure that qualitative text analysis will face methodical improvements in the near future because of the great interest in this form of systematic analysis.

Finally, it must be noted that qualitative text analysis is a method that is characterized by the fact that the research question is of central importance throughout the entire analysis process. Qualitative text analysis enables you to anchor the empirical results of your research and develop and test your theories based on the data.

References

Bailey, K. D. (1973). Monothetic and Polythetic Typologies and their Relation to Conceptualization, Measurement and Scaling. *American Sociological Review, 38*(1), 18–33.

Bailey, K. D. (1994). *Typology and Taxonomies. An Introduction to Classification Techniques*. Thousand Oaks, CA: Sage Publications.

Barton, A. H. (1955). The Concept of Property-space in Social Research. In P. F. Lazarsfeld & M. Rosenberg (eds), *The Language of Social Research* (pp. 40–53). New York: Free Press.

Bazeley, P. (2007). *Qualitative Data Analysis with NVivo*. Thousand Oaks, CA: Sage Publications.

Berelson, B. (1952). *Content Analysis in Communication Research*. Glencoe: Free Press.

Berelson, B., & Lazarsfeld, P. F. (1948). *The Analysis of Communication Content*. Chicago: University of Chicago.

Bernard, H. R., & Ryan, G. W. (2010). *Analyzing Qualitative Data. Systematic Approaches*. Thousand Oaks, CA: Sage Publications.

Boyatzis, R. E. (1998). *Transforming Qualitative Information: Thematic Analysis and Code Development*. Thousand Oaks, CA: Sage Publications.

Bryman, A. (1988). *Quantity and Quality in Social Research*. London: Routledge.

Charmaz, K. (2006). *Constructing Grounded Theory: A Practical Guide Through Qualitative Analysis*. Thousand Oaks, CA: Sage Publications.

Charmaz, K. (2011). Grounded Theory Methods in Social Justice Research. In N. K. Denzin & Y. Lincoln (eds), *The SAGE Handbook of Qualitative Research* (4th ed., pp. 359–380). Thousand Oaks, CA: Sage Publications.

Charmaz, K., & Bryant, A. (eds). (2007). *The SAGE Handbook of Grounded Theory*. Thousand Oaks, CA: Sage Publications.

Cisneros-Puebla, C. A. (2004). 'To Learn to Think Conceptually'. Juliet Corbin in Conversation With Cesar A. Cisneros-Puebla [53 paragraphs]. *Forum Qualitative Sozialforschung / Forum: Qualitative Social Research, 5*(3), Art. 32. Retrieved 28.03.13, from http://nbn-resolving.de/urn:nbn:de:0114-fqs0403325

Clarke, A. (2005). *Situational Analysis: Grounded Theory After the Postmodern Turn*. Thousand Oaks, CA: Sage Publications.

Corbin, J., & Strauss, A. L. (2008). *Basics of Qualitative Research: Grounded Theory Procedures and Techniques* (3rd ed.). Thousand Oaks, CA: Sage Publications.

Creswell, J. W. (2003). *Research Design. Qualitative, Quantitative, and Mixed Methods Approaches*. Thousand Oaks, CA: Sage Publications.

Creswell, J. W. (2007). *Qualitative Inquiry and Research Design. Choosing Among Five Approaches*. Thousand Oaks, CA: Sage Publications.

Creswell, J. W. (2009). *Research Design: Qualitative, Quantitative, and Mixed Methods Approaches* (3rd ed.). Thousand Oaks, CA: Sage Publications.

Creswell, J. W., & Plano Clark, V. L. (2011). *Designing and Conducting Mixed Methods Research* (2nd ed.). Thousand Oaks, CA: Sage Publications.

Danner, H. (2006). *Methoden geisteswissenschaftlicher Pädagogik* (5th ed.). München: Utb.

Denzin, N. K. (1978). *The Research Act: A Theoretical Introduction to Sociological Methods* (2nd ed.). New York: McGraw Hill.

Denzin, N. K., & Lincoln, Y. (2011). Preface. In N. Denzin & Y. Lincoln (eds.), *The SAGE Handbook of Qualitative Research* (4th ed., pp. ix–xvi). Thousand Oaks, CA: Sage Publications.

Dey, I. (1993). *Qualitative Data Analysis: A User-Friendly Guide for Social Scientists.* London: Routledge.

Diekmann, A. (2007). *Empirische Sozialforschung. Grundlagen, Methoden, Anwendungen* (18th ed.). Reinbek bei Hamburg: Rowohlt.

Dresing, T., Pehl, T., & Schmieder, C. (2013). Manual (on) Transcription. Transcription Conventions, Software Guides and Practical Hints for Qualitative Researchers 2nd Edition. Retrieved 10.04.13, from http://www.audiotranskription.de/english/transcription-practicalguide.htm

Feyerabend, P. (1975). *Against Method: Outline of an Anarchistic Theory of Knowledge.* Atlantic Highlands, N.J.: Humanities Press.

Fielding, J. (2008). 'Double Whammy? Are the Most at Risk the Least Aware?' A study of Environmental Justice and Awareness of Flood Risk in England and Wales. In W. Allsop, P. Samuels, J. Harrop & S. Huntington (eds), *Flood Risk Management: Research and Practice.* London: Taylor and Frances.

Fielding, N., & Lee, R. (1998). *Computer Analysis and Qualitative Research.* Thousand Oaks, CA: Sage Publications.

Flick, U. (2006). *An Introduction to Qualitative Research* (3rd ed.). London: Sage Publications.

Flick, U. (2007a). *Qualitative Sozialforschung. Eine Einführung.* Reinbek bei Hamburg: Rowohlt.

Flick, U. (2007b). *Triangulation. Eine Einführung* (2nd ed.). Wiesbaden: VS Verlag.

Flick, U. (2009). *Sozialforschung. Methoden und Anwendungen. Ein Überblick für die BA-Studiengänge.* Reinbek bei Hamburg: Rowohlt.

Flick, U., von Kardorff, E., & Steinke, I. (eds). (2004). *A Companion to Qualitative Research.* London: Sage Publications.

Frueh, W. (2004). *Inhaltsanalyse. Theorie und Praxis* (5th ed.). Konstanz: UVK.

Gadamer, H.-G. (1972). *Wahrheit und Methode. Grundzüge einer philosophischen Hermeneutik.* Tübingen: J.C.B. Mohr Verlag.

Gadamer, H.-G. (2004). *Truth and Method.* London: Continuum Publishing.

Gibbs, G. R. (2009). *Analysing Qualitative Data.* Thousand Oaks, CA: Sage Publications.

Glaeser, J., & Laudel, G. (2010). *Experteninterviews und qualitative Inhaltsanalyse: Als Instrumente rekonstruierender Untersuchungen* (4th ed.). Wiesbaden: VSVerlag.

Glaser, B. G., & Strauss, A. L. (1967). *The Discovery of Grounded Theory.* Chicago: Aldine.

Glaser, B. G., & Strauss, A. L. (1998). *Grounded Theory. Strategien qualitativer Forschung.* Bern: Huber.

Guba, E., & Lincoln, Y. S. (1985). *Naturalistic Inquiry.* Thousand Oaks, CA: Sage Publications.

Guest, G., MaxQueen, K., & Namey, E. (2012). *Applied Thematic Analysis.* Thousand Oaks, CA: Sage Publications.

Hammersley, M. (1992). *What's Wrong with Ethnography? Methodological Explorations.* London: Routledge.

Hempel, C. G., & Oppenheim, P. (1936). *Der Typusbegriff im Lichte der neuen Logik. Wissenschaftstheoretische Untersuchungen zur Konstitutionsforschung und Psychologie.* Leiden: Sijthoff Verlag.

Hopf, C., Rieker, P., Sanden-Marcus, M., & Schmidt, C. (1995). *Familie und Rechtsextremismus. Familiale Sozialisation und rechtsextreme Orientierungen junger Männer.* Weinheim: Juventa.

Hopf, C., & Schmidt, C. (1993). Zum Verhältnis von innerfamilialen sozialen Erfahrungen, Persönlichkeitsentwicklung und politischen Orientierungen. Hildesheim: Institut für Sozialwissenschaften der Universität Hildesheim.

Huberman, A. M., & Miles, M. B. (1994). *Qualitative Data Analysis. An Expanded Sourcebook* (2nd ed.). Thousand Oaks, CA: Sage Publications.

Jahoda, M., Lazarsfeld, P. F., & Zeisel, H. (1975). *Die Arbeitslosen von Marienthal. Ein soziographischer Versuch* (1st ed.). Frankfurt/M.: Suhrkamp.

Jahoda, M., Lazarsfeld, P. F., & Zeisel, H. (2002). *Marienthal. The Sociography of an Unemployed Community. With a new introduction by Christian Fleck.* New Brunswick, N.J.; London: Transaction Publishers.

Jefferson, G. (1984). Transcription Notation. In J. Atkinson & J. Heritags (eds), *Structures of Social Interaction.* New York: Cambridge University Press.

Kelle, U. (2007a). The Development of Categories: Different Approaches in Grounded Theory. In A. Bryant & K. Charmaz (eds), *The Sage Handbook of Grounded Theory* (pp. 191–213). London: Sage.

Kelle, U. (2007b). *Die Integration qualitativer und quantitativer Methoden in der empirischen Sozialforschung. Theoretische Grundlagen und methodologische Konzepte.* Wiesbaden: VS Verlag.

Kelle, U. (2007c). 'Emergence' vs. 'Forcing' of Empirical Data? A Crucial Problem of 'Grounded Theory' Reconsidered. In G. Mey & K. Mruck (eds), *Grounded Theory Reader* (pp. 133–155). Köln: Zentrum für Historische Sozialforschung.

Kelle, U., & Kluge, S. (eds). (2010). *Vom Einzelfall zum Typus. Fallvergleich und Fallkontrastierung in der qualitativen Sozialforschung* (2nd ed.). Wiesbaden: VS Verlag.

Kelle, U., Prein, G., & Bird, K. (1995). *Computer-Aided Qualitative Data Analysis: Theory, Methods and Practice.* Thousand Oaks, CA: Sage Publications.

Kirk, J., & Miller, M. L. (1986). *Reliability and Validity in Qualitative Research.* Thousand Oaks, CA: Sage Publications.

Klafki, W. (2001)[1971]. Hermeneutische Verfahren in der Erziehungswissenschaft. In C. Rittelmeyer & M. Parmentier (eds), *Einführung in die pädagogische Hermeneutik. Mit einem Beitrag von Wolfgang Klafki.* (pp. 125–148). Darmstadt: Wissenschaftliche Buchgesellschaft.

Kluge, S. (1999). *Empirisch begründete Typenbildung. Zur Konstruktion von Typen und Typologien in der qualitativen Sozialforschung.* Opladen: Leske & Budrich.

Kluge, S. (2000). Empirically Grounded Construction of Types and Typologies in Qualitative Social Research [14 paragraphs]. *Forum Qualitative Sozialforschung / Forum: Qualitative Social Research, 1*(1), Art. 14. Retrieved 10.04.13, from http://nbn-resolving.de/urn:nbn:de:0114-fqs0001145

Kowal, S., & O'Connell, D. C. (2004). The Transcription of Conversations. In U. Flick, E. von Kardorff & I. Steinke (eds), *A Companion to Qualitative Research* (pp. 248–252). London: Sage Publications.

Kracauer, S. (1952). The Challenge of Qualitative Content Analysis. *Public Opinion Quarterly, 16*, 631–642.

Krippendorff, K. (2004). *Content Analysis. An Introduction to Its Methodology* (2nd ed.). Thousand Oaks, CA: Sage Publications.

Kriz, J., & Lisch, R. (1988). *Methoden-Lexikon*. Weinheim/München: PVU.

Kuckartz, U. (1991). Ideal Types or Empirical Types: The Case of Max Weber's Empirical Research. *Bulletin de Méthodologie Sociologique, 32*(1), 44–53.

Kuckartz, U. (2009). Methodenkombination. In B. Westle (ed.), *Methoden der Politikwissenschaft* (pp. 352–362). Baden-Baden: Nomos.

Kuckartz, U. (2010a). *Einführung in die computergestützte Analyse qualitativer Daten* (3rd ed.). Wiesbaden: VS Verlag.

Kuckartz, U. (2010b). Nicht hier, nicht jetzt, nicht ich – Über die symbolische Bearbeitung eines ernsthaften Problems. In H. W. u.a. (ed.), *Klimakulturen. Soziale Wirklichkeiten im Klimawandel* (pp. 144–160). Frankfurt: Campus.

Kuckartz, U. (2010c). Type-bildung. In G. Mey & K. Mruck (eds), *Handbuch Qualitative Forschung in der Psychologie* (pp. 553–568). Wiesbaden: VS Verlag.

Kuckartz, U., Dresing, T., Raediker, S., & Stefer, C. (2008). *Qualitative Evaluation. Der Einstieg in die Praxis* (2nd ed.). Wiesbaden: VS Verlag.

Lamnek, S. (1993). *Methoden und Techniken*. Weinheim: PVU.

Lamnek, S. (2005). *Qualitative Sozialforschung. Lehrbuch* (4th ed.). Weinheim: Beltz.

Lazarsfeld, P. F. (1972). *Qualitative Analysis. Historical and Critical Essays*. Boston: Allyn and Bacon.

Legewie, H., & Schervier-Legewie, B. (2004). 'Research is Hard Work, it's Always a Bit suffering. Therefore on the Other Side it Should be Fun'. Anselm Strauss in conversation with Heiner Legewie and Barbara Schervier-Legewie. *Forum Qualitative Sozialforschung / Forum: Qualitative Social Research, 5*(3), Art. 22. Retrieved 28.03.13, from http://nbn-resolving.de/urn:nbn:de:0114-fqs0403222

Lewins, A., & Silver, C. (2007). *Using Software in Qualitative Research: A Step-By-Step Guide*. Thousand Oaks, CA: Sage Publications.

Mackie, J. L. (1974). *The Cement of the Universe. A Study of Causation*. Oxford: Clarendon Press.

Marshall, C., & Rossman, G. B. (2006). *Designing Qualitative Research* (4th ed.). Thousand Oaks, CA: Sage Publications.

Mayring, P. (2000). Qualitative Content Analysis [28 paragraphs]. *Forum Qualitative Sozialforschung / Forum: Qualitative Social Research, 1*(2), Art. 20. Retrieved 28.03.13, from http://nbn-resolving.de/urn:nbn:de:0114-fqs0002204

Mayring, P. (2010). *Qualitative Inhaltsanalyse. Grundlagen und Techniken* (1st ed.). Weinheim: Beltz.

Mayring, P., & Glaeser-Zikuda, M. (2005). *Die Praxis der qualitativen Inhaltsanalyse*. Weinheim: Beltz.

Merten, K. (1995). *Inhaltsanalyse. Einführung in Theorie, Methode und Praxis* (2nd ed.). Opladen: Westdeutscher Verlag.

Miles, M. B., & Huberman, A. M. (1995). *Qualitative Data Analysis. An Expanded Sourcebook* (2nd ed.). Thousand Oaks, CA: Sage Publications.

Miller, D. C., & Salkind, N. J. (2002). *Handbook of Research Design and Social Measurement* (6th ed.). Thousand Oaks, CA: Sage Publications.

Mollenhauer, K., & Uhlendorff, U. (1992). Zur Methode der hermeneutisch-diagnostischen Interpretation *Sozialpädagogische Diagnosen* (pp. 28–35). Weinheim: Beltz.

Oswald, H. (2010). Was heißt qualitativ forschen? Warnungen, Fehlerquellen, Möglichkeiten. In B. Friebertshaeuser, A. Langer & A. Prengel (eds), *Handbuch qualitative Forschungsmethoden in der Erziehungswissenschaft* (3rd ed., pp. 183–201). Weinheim: Juventa.

Preisendoerfer, P. (1999). *Umwelteinstellungen und Umweltverhalten in Deutschland. Empirische Befunde und Analysen auf der Grundlage der Bevölkerungsumfragen 'Umweltbewußtsein in Deutschland 1991–1998'.* Opladen: Leske & Budrich.

Rasmussen, E. S., Østergaard, P., & Beckmann, S. C. (2006). *Essentials of Social Science Research Methodology.* Odense: University Press of Southern Denmark.

Richards, L., & Richards, T. (1994). Using Computers in Qualitative Research. In N. K. Denzin & Y. S. Lincoln (eds), *Handbook Qualitative Research* (pp. 445–462). Thousand Oaks, CA: Sage Publications.

Ritchie, J., & Spencer, L. (1994). Qualitative Data Analysis for Applied Policy Research. In A. Bryman & R. Burgess (eds), *Analyzing Qualitative Data* (pp. 173–194). London: Routledge.

Ritchie, J., Spencer, L., & O'Connor, W. (2003). Carrying out Qualitative Analysis. In J. Ritchie & J. Lewis (eds), *Qualitative Research Practice: A Guide for Social Science Students and Researchers* (pp. 219–261). Thousand Oaks, CA: Sage Publications.

Roessler, P. (2005). *Inhaltsanalyse.* Konstanz: UVK.

Rorty, R. (1979). *Philosophy and the Mirror of Nature.* Princeton: Princeton University Press.

Schmidt, C. (2000). Analyse von Leitfadeninterviews. In U. Flick, E. v. Kardoff & I. Steinke (eds), *Qualitative Forschung. Ein Handbuch* (pp. 447–455). Reinbek bei Hamburg: Rowohlt.

Schmidt, C. (2010). Auswertungstechniken für Leitfadeninterviews. In B. Friebertshaeuser, A. Langer & A. Prengel (eds), *Handbuch qualitative Forschungsmethoden in der Erziehungswissenschaft* (3rd ed., pp. 473–486). Weinheim: Juventa.

Schnell, R., Hill, P. B., & Esser, E. (2008). *Methoden der empirischen Sozialforschung* (8th ed.). München: Oldenbourg.

Schreier, M. (2012). *Qualitative Content Analysis in Practice.* London: Sage Publications.

Schuetz, A. (1972). *Gesammelte Aufsätze.* Den Haag: Nijhoff.

Schutz, A. (1972). *Collected Papers I: The Problem of Social Reality.* Edited by M. A. Natanson and H. L. van Breda. Dordrecht, The Netherlands: Martinus Nijhoff Publishers.

Seale, C. (1999a). Quality in Qualitative Research. *Qualitative Inquiry, 5*(4), 465–478.

Seale, C. (1999b). *The Quality of Qualitative Research.* Thousand Oaks, CA: Sage Publications.

Seale, C., & Silverman, D. (1997). Ensuring rigour in qualitative research. *European Journal of Public Health, H.7,* 379–384.

Spencer, L., Ritchie, J., Lewis, J., & Dillon, L. (2003). *Quality in Qualitative Evaluation: A Framework for Assessing Research Evidence.* London: Government Chief Social Researcher's Office, The Cabinet Office.

Sprenger, A. (1989). Teilnehmende Beobachtung in prekären Handlungssituationen. Das Beispiel Intensivstation. In R. Aster, H. Merkens & M. Repp (eds), *Teilnehmende Beobachtung. Werkstattberichte und methodologische Reflexionen* (pp. 35–57). Frankfurt/Main: Campus.

Steinke, I. (2004). Quality Criteria in Qualitative Research. In U. Flick, E. Von Kardorff & I. Steinke (eds), *A Companion to Qualitative Research* (pp. 184–190). London: Sage Publications.

Strauss, A. L. (1987). *Qualitative Analysis for Social Scientists*. Cambridge: Cambridge University Press.

Strauss, A. L. (1991). *Grundlagen qualitativer Sozialforschung: Datenanalyse und Theoriebildung in der empirischen soziologischen Forschung*. München: Fink.

Strauss, A. L., & Corbin, J. M. (1996). *Grounded Theory. Grundlagen qualitativer Sozialforschung*. Weinheim: Beltz.

Strauss, A. L., & Corbin, J.M. (1998). *Basics of Qualitative Research: Techniques and Procedures for Developing Grounded Theory* (2nd ed.). Thousand Oaks, CA: Sage Publications.

Tashakkori, A., & Teddlie, C. (2010). *SAGE Handbook of Mixed Methods in Social & Behavioral Research* (2nd ed.). Thousand Oaks, CA: Sage Publications.

Teddlie, C., & Tashakkori, A. (2009). *Foundations of Mixed Methods Research: Integrating Quantitative and Qualitative Approaches in the Social and Behavioral Sciences*. Thousand Oaks, CA: Sage Publications.

Tesch, R. (1992). *Qualitative Research. Analysis Types and Software Tools*. New York: Palmer Press.

Vogt, J. (2008). Vorlesung zur Hermeneutik. *Buch: Einladung zur Literaturwissenschaft, Vertiefung im Internet*. Retrieved from http://www.uni-duisburg-essen.de/literatur-wissenschaft-aktiv/Vorlesungen/hermeneutik/main.html

Weber, M. (1911). Geschäftsbericht auf dem 1. Deutschen Soziologentag vom 19. – 22.10.1910 in Frankfurt/Main. *Verhandlungen der Deutschen Soziologentage, Tübingen. Stuttgart: Enke, 39–52.*

Weber, M. (1978). *Economy and Society: An Outline of Interpretative Sociology (2 volume set)*. Edited by G. Roth & C. Wittich. Berkeley & Los Angeles: University California Press.

Weitzman, E. A., & Miles, M. B. (1995). *Computer Programs for Qualitative Data Analysis. A Software Sourcebook*. Thousand Oaks, CA: Sage Publications.

Wenzler-Cremer, H. (2005). Bikulturelle Sozialisation als Herausforderung und Chance. Eine qualitative Studie über Identitätskonstruktionen und Lebensentwürfe am Beispiel junger deutsch-indonesischer Frauen. Retrieved from http://www.freidok.uni-freiburg.de/volltexte/2267/pdf/Bikulturelle_Sozialisation.pdf

Witzel, A. (2000). The Problem-Centered Interview [26 paragraphs]. *Forum Qualitative Sozialforschung / Forum: Qualitative Social Research, 1*(1), Art. 22. Retrieved 18.10.11, from http://nbn-resolving.de/urn:nbn:de:0114-fqs0001228

Yarbrough, D. B., Shulha, L. M., Hopson, R. K., & Caruthers, F. A. (2011). *The Program Evaluation Standards: A Guide for Evaluators and Evaluation Users* (3rd ed.). Thousand Oaks, CA: Sage Publications.

Zuell, C., & Mohler, P. P. (eds). (1992). *Textanalyse. Anwendungen der computergestützten Inhaltsanalyse*. Opladen: Westdeutscher Verlag.

Index

Page references to Figures or Tables will be in *italics*